INVISIBLE BOUNDARIES

The EFPP Series

Editors in Chief: *Monica Lanyado and Didier Houzel*
Associate Editors: *Brian Martindale* (Adult Section)
Didier Houzel (Child and Adolescent Section)
Alessandro Bruni (Group Section)

OTHER TITLES IN THE SERIES

- *Countertransference in Psychoanalytic Psychotherapy with Children and Adolescents*
- *Supervision and its Vicissitudes*
- *Psychoanalytic Psychotherapy in Institutional Settings*
- *Psychoanalytic Psychotherapy of the Severely Disturbed Adolescent*
- *Work with Parents: Psychoanalytic Psychotherapy with Children and Adolescents*
- *Psychoanalysis and Psychotherapy: The Controversies and the Future*
- *Research on Psychoanalytic Psychotherapy with Adults*
- *The Therapist at Work: Personal Factors Affecting the Analytic Process*

INVISIBLE BOUNDARIES

Psychosis and autism in children and adolescents

Edited by

Didier Houzel and Maria Rhode

Routledge
Taylor & Francis Group
LONDON AND NEW YORK

for

The European Federation
for Psychoanalytic Psychotherapy
in the Public Health Services
and
The Cyprus Association
for Psychoanalytic Psychotherapy Studies

First published 2005 by Karnac Books Ltd.

2 Park Square, Milton Park, Abingdon, Oxfordshire OX14 4RN
52 Vanderbilt Avenue, New York, NY 10017

Routledge is an imprint of the Taylor & Francis Group, an informa business

First issued in hardback 2019

Chapter 3 'The symbolic and the concrete: psychotic adolescents in psychoanalytic psychotherapy', by Julia Pestalozzi, reprinted from the *International Journal of Psychoanalysis, 84* (2003): 733–753 with the permission of the publisher.

British Library Cataloguing in Publication Data

A C.I.P. for this book is available from the British Library

ISBN 978-1-85575-398-3 (pbk)
ISBN 978-0-367-32518-3 (hbk)

Edited, designed, and produced by The Studio Publishing Services Ltd, Exeter EX4 8JN

CONTENTS

To the memory of Frances Tustin

EDITORS AND CONTRIBUTORS

ANNE ALVAREZ (UK) is a lecturer at the Tavistock Clinic in London, where she recently retired as Consultant Child and Adolescent Psychotherapist and co-convenor of the Autism Service. She is the author of *Live Company: Psychotherapy with Autistic, Borderline, Deprived and Abused Children* (Routledge, 1992) and co-editor of *Autism and Personality: Findings from the Tavistock Autism Worshop* (Alvarez & Reid: Routledge, 1999). She has published many papers on psychoanalytic psychotherapy with autistic, borderline and traumatized patients. A book of her seminars at the Brazilian Psychoanalytic Society, *Anne Alvarez in Sao Paolo,* was published in 1999, and a festschrift, *Being Alive: Building on the Work of Anne Alvarez* (Ed. Judith Edwards, Routledge) in 2002.

BRITTA BLOMBERG (Sweden), licensed psychologist, licensed psychotherapist and trained supervisor, is a child and adolescent psychotherapist, supervisor and teacher at the Erica Foundation in Stockholm. She is a member of the Swedish Association for Child and Adolescent Psychotherapy and a Swedish delegate for the EFPP (Child and Adolescent Section). She is the founder and Editor of *Mellanrummet: Journal of Child and Adolescent Psychotherapy.*

RAYMOND CAHN (France) is a psychiatrist and psychoanalyst, and *membre titulaire* of the Paris Psychoanalytic Society, of which he was President in 1979–1980. For many years he has served on the editorial committees of the journals *Revue Française de Psychanalyse* and *Adolescence*. He has been Medical Director of an important day hospital in Paris for adolescents (CEREP). His theoretical work is mainly about the psychopathology of adolescence and the process subjectivation, i.e., the psychic process that leads the individual to acknowledge his/her personal identity as a subject.

GENEVIÈVE HAAG (France) is a child psychiatrist and psychoanalyst. She is a member of the Paris Psychoanalytical Society. She has worked with several Kleinian psychoanalysts, in particular James Gammill, Frances Tustin and Esther Bick. She was the first to introduce, with her husband Dr Michel Haag, Esther Bick's method of infant observation in France in the late 1970s. She has published many articles on psychotic and autistic children and specializes in the problem of the body image and its profound distortions in her clinical and theoretical work.

DIDIER HOUZEL (France) is Professor of Child and Adolescent Psychiatry at the University of Caen. He is a Full Member of the French Psychoanalytic Association. He has worked with several Kleinian psychoanalysts, in particular James Gammill in Paris, Donald Meltzer in London and the late Frances Tustin in Amersham. In collaboration with Didier Anzieu, he has published papers on psychic envelopes. He has also published several psychoanalytic articles on autism and childhood psychoses. He is President of the French Federation for Child and Adolescent Psychoanalytic Psychotherapy affiliated to the European Federation for Psychoanalytic Psychotherapy in the Public Sector.

SUZANNE MAIELLO (Italy) is in psychoanalytic practice with children and adults in Rome (Italy). She is a member of the ACP, founder member and past-President of AIPPI (Italian Association of Psychoanalytic Child Psychotherapy), a teacher and supervisor in the Tavistock Model AIPPI Infant Observation and Child Psychotherapy Training, and a member of the teaching staff for the MA in Observational Studies at the University of East London. Co-author of numerous books, she has published worldwide in the leading journals of child psychotherapy and psychoanalysis. Her special field of interest is the relation between prenatal auditory experience and proto-mental activity and between prenatal and perinatal trauma and autistic states. She was the first recipient of the International Frances Tustin Memorial Prize.

FRANÇOIS MARTY (France) is a psychologist and psychoanalyst. He is Professor of Psychology at the University René Descartes in Paris. He is Director in that university of the Laboratory of Clinical Psychology and Psychopathology. He is President of the International College of Adolescence (CILA). He is a specialist on the psychopathology of adolescence, about which he has published several books.

MARIA RHODE (UK) is Professor of Child Psychotherapy at the Tavistock Clinic and the University of East London. She has lectured and published widely on autistic spectrum disorders, language development, and infant observation, and is co-editor of *Psychotic States in Children* (Rustin, Rhode, Dubinsky, & Dubinsky, Duckworth, 1997) and *The Many Faces of Asperger's Syndrome* (Rhode & Klauber, Karnac, 2004). She is currently working on an early intervention project for toddlers with communication difficulties.

JULIA PESTALOZZI (Switzerland) qualified in clinical psychology in Budapest, in medicine in London, and specialized in psychiatry and psychotherapy for children and adolescents in Switzerland. She lives in Basel and works as a psychoanalyst, psychoanalytic psychotherapist, and supervisor in private practice. Her main interest lies in the field of psychoanalytic psychotherapy of psychoses, particularly of adolescents. She is a former member of the EFPP executive board.

SERIES EDITORS' PREFACE

This volume of contributions about psychotic and autistic conditions in childhood and adolescence, by internationally distinguished psychoanalytic clinicians, offers an original perspective on this difficult and at times contentious subject. The book is an outcome of the EFPP (European Federation for Psychoanalytic Psychotherapy) conference held on the subject in Caen, France, in 2001, and embodies the central aim of the EFPP and this book series, to encourage the cross-fertilization of psychoanalytic practice and theory across the international boundaries in Europe.

We are pleased to be able to claim that this collection of papers and interviews with major thinkers in this area of work is one of the first "post-Tustin" books on work with child and adolescent patients with psychosis and autism of which we are aware. Most of the contributors were either supervised by Tustin or profoundly influenced by her work. Each of them has creatively built on this influence. We are particularly pleased to include in this volume interviews with Geneviève Haag and Raymond Cahn, whose highly influential work has so far not been widely translated into English. As Tustin delighted in encouraging the international sharing of ideas, this volume is very much a development of her work.

To continue the theme of cross-fertilization, as Houzel and Rhode emphasize in their introduction, with the advent of new techniques of brain imaging, and the important and rapidly expanding researches in neurophysiology and developmental psychology, there is no longer an incompatibility between psychoanalytic understandings and biological researches. The aetiology of psychotic and autistic conditions in childhood and adolescence is now more usually understood as being multi-factorial. The contributors to this volume clearly find the work of their colleagues in the neurosciences extremely helpful and use it productively in their understanding of patients clinically and theoretically. It is important to note that this sharing ideas and communication across disciplines is mutually rewarding, as psychoanalytic insights based on detailed and in depth clinical work with these patients is also of great value to our colleagues in the neurosciences.

We hope that the reader will enjoy this volume and be stimulated by its international flavour to join us at future conferences—or if this is not possible, enjoy the fruits of the conferences in other publications in this series.

Monica Lanyado and Didier Houzel
Series Editors

Introduction

Didier Houzel and Maria Rhode

The psychoanalytic approach to childhood psychosis was a cornerstone of the work of clinicians as various as Melanie Klein and Margaret Mahler. Despite the difficulty of the work, the incredulity of many and the vehement opposition of some, psychoanalytic workers continue to offer treatment and support to these most severely afflicted children and adolescents and to their families. And, indeed, opposition to a psychoanalytic approach tends to address positions that are now outdated.

The time is past when certain psychoanalysts stigmatized parents as "schizophrenogenic" (Fromm-Reichmann, 1950) or as causing other kinds of psychotic disturbance (Bettelheim, 1967). It took a long time for psychoanalysts to realize that their science did not concern aetiology, that is, that they were not in a position to detect the causes of the psychological difficulties they treated. Psychoanalysis seeks to understand the meaning of symptoms, not their cause. There exists, therefore, no incompatibility whatsoever between psychoanalysis and the research of biologists (geneticists, biochemists, neurophysiologists) or of cognitive scientists. Biologists and cognitive scientists look for causes; psychoanalysts look for meaning. Each line of enquiry follows a carefully defined methodology corresponding to its own epistemological position. It would be wrong to be surprised at the existence of more than one point of view: that would mean ignoring the need for "complex thought", in Edgar Morin's (1991) terms; that is, the need to explore some phenomena by approaching them by different means, from different perspectives, all of which are complementary and none of which is primary.

The contribution of psychoanalysis to the exploration of psychotic phenomena is necessarily limited. It has no claim to being exclusive: the relevance of the biological sciences is beyond dispute, and these allow investigation both of risk factors and of brain mechanisms. Equally, cognitive science allows us to refine our understanding of those information processing strategies that are characteristic of psychotic states. As far as children are concerned, it is through developmental research that the contributions of biology and of cognitive science become relevant. Several of the authors in this volume refer extensively to the developmentalists' contributions; and these contributions have themselves influenced therapeutic approaches and technique. There is real scope for cross-fertilization based on mutual respect and on the absence of any claim to exclusive importance.

Like many other workers, we feel that a multi-factorial aetiology is the most convincing. Whatever the aetiology may be, even a purely organic defect would not be an argument against a psychological approach. Someone whose way of being is different from other people's will benefit from help in understanding how this impinges on them. Understanding and managing the emotional ramifications can allow them to make the fullest possible use of their capacities. For example, Valerie Sinason has illustrated the impact of therapy on people with learning disabilities, which are frequently organically determined. However, this irreducible "primary handicap" (Sinason, 1986) is often greatly augmented by an emotionally-based "secondary handicap" which can be significantly influenced by psychotherapy (see also Simpson & Miller (2004), *Unexpected Gains*). Similarly, Grotstein (1997) has proposed that the effect of psychotherapy on patients with an autistic spectrum disorder may come about through helping them to manage their condition.

Quite apart from such issues, recent research increasingly suggests that the long-standing dichotomy between organicist and psychodynamic views may turn out to be a false one. The development of new techniques of brain imaging is making it possible to correlate emotional experiences with brain chemistry, physiology and anatomy (Damasio, 2000; Kaplan-Solms & Solms 2000; Perry, Pollard, Blakely, Baker, & Vigilante, 1995; Schore 1994, 2001a,b; Solms & Turnbull 2002). Schore (1994, 2001a,b), for example, has reviewed a great body of neurophysiological work investigating brain activity in mother–infant pairs. His conclusion is that the regulation of babies' emotions that takes place within their relationship with a responsive caregiver can be understood in terms of the immediate resonance between neurophysiological activity in the right brain hemispheres of the two members of the dyad. With neurophysiological patterns in the right hemisphere of each member reflecting those in the right hemisphere of the other, the caregiver resonates to the baby's emotions, modulates them, and the baby in turn resonates to the caregiver's modulated levels of arousal. Important brain circuits are often not adequately established in children who have suffered serious deprivation with regard to satisfying social interactions. Early traumatic experience, on the other hand, can lead to the over-use of neural pathways concerned with overwhelming fear responses. One consequence of this is that relatively mild unpleasant stimuli can travel down these "super-highway" paths and trigger responses that are much more extreme than the stimulus would normally provoke. (For a helpful review, see Balbernie, 2001.) None of this is an argument against the idea that a brain defect may be present from birth in children later diagnosed with a psychotic disorder. It is, however, a strong argument against regarding such a brain defect as being unmodifiable.

Like the interaction between baby and caregiver, the interaction between patient and therapist involves emotional resonance and modulation, and therefore the possibility of the modification of brain structure and function. This is not to suggest that long-established neurological pathways can be made redundant, or that inbuilt or long-standing neurological deficits can be made good. What can happen, however, is that higher-order pathways can be laid down that make it possible to manage experiences that would previously have been overwhelming (Schore, 2002). The correspondence is obvious between this neurological formulation and Bion's (1962) model of the containing function.

The importance of this line of thought can hardly be overstated in relation to psychotherapy for conditions involving a neurological element. Even where neurologically-based difficulties may persist, patients can grow to look after them better, and their experience of other people and of themselves can be transformed. This, incidentally, is also true of people who have psychotherapy for other kinds of difficulty. Probably every patient—and therapist—at length comes to realize that aspects of their endowment and experience are there to stay. What can be changed, often dramatically, is the way these aspects are managed and integrated, and, by this means, the way they impact upon a person's life.

Some readers may be surprised at the inclusion of papers on autism (Kanner, 1943) or Asperger's Syndrome (Asperger, 1944) under the general heading of *Psychosis in Childhood and Adolescence.* In some countries, the term "psychosis" is not used with regard to children. It does not appear in *ICD-10* (1993) or in the American classificatory system of *DSM-IV* (1994). This, in fact, is a purely semantic and nosographical problem, and should not be allowed to obscure clinical facts. The French classificatory system for disturbances in childhood and adolescence retains the terms "psychosis" and "psychotic" with respect to children for the description of conditions which the other classifications designate as "atypical autism". What matters is that these variously named clinical pictures correspond, as is the case; and that the terms "psychosis" and "autism" should not imply any aetiological assumptions. A whole line of critical argument has developed according to which "psychosis" is considered as a mental illness, while "autism" is seen as a constitutional impairment rather than as a "mental illness". This argument seems insecurely based. It is important to remember that, so far, there is no conclusive evidence concerning the aetiology either of autism or of psychotic conditions. In the clinical setting, children may frequently be seen to develop a post-autistic psychosis (Haag, 1997; Meltzer, Bremner, Hoxter, Weddell, & Wittenberg, 1975); equally, autism can serve as a strait-jacket which holds psychosis in check (Rhode, 1997; Tustin, 1990, 1994). Recent research has yielded a rich harvest of results concerning the disturbances of brain function and the atypical cognitive strategies that may be observed both in autism and in psychosis. However, since none of these disturbances or anomalies can explain all the observed phenomena, they cannot rightly be regarded as aetiological factors.[1]

The phenomena, then, are beyond question, but they remain difficult to interpret. Do they reflect causal factors? Are they a manifestation of the disturbance? Are they a sign of processes in the brain that mediate the particular behaviours of people with the condition being studied, without being the cause of these? A scientific stance implies modesty: it recognizes how much remains unknown and unexplored—usually far more than has been mapped. It involves respect for the degree of uncertainty involved in the investigation of the severe early psychological disturbances that form the subject matter of this volume. However these may be characterized, they interfere with individuation and with the recognition of otherness. To a greater or lesser extent, they jeopardize the sense of reality, and profoundly affect the capacity to communicate with one's fellows and to take one's place amongst them.

Anne Alvarez's contribution, "Autism and psychosis", reflects her long experience in treating autistic and psychotic children and adolescents. It reflects also her profound understanding of the implications of recent developmental research for the understanding of psychopathology, as well as of psychoanalytic theory itself. The originality of her work, as shown in her book, *Live Company*, has made her one of the leading exponents of the psychoanalysis of autistic and psychotic children. She has extended the work of Frances Tustin, particularly in matters of technique, where she emphasizes the importance of "reclaiming" the child by actively intervening to help him to relinquish stereotypic behaviour in favour of communication. Her present contribution focuses on deficits in the autistic child's internal objects. By this we must understand a failure to introject the containing function, whatever factors may have entered into the child's atypical development. Alvarez is concerned to build bridges between her own psychoanalytic framework and the biological and cognitivist framework of developmental researchers. For example, she links impaired introjection to anomalies of neurological arousal thresholds, and the psychoanalytic concept of defence to neurophysiological models of regulation. There is always the danger that syncretism could undermine the epistemological validity of concepts that arose in one field through their uncritical application to another. Alvarez's open-minded thinking avoids this danger, while drawing on the richness of an ongoing dialectic between levels of discourse—intersubjective, intrasubjective, and cognitive aspects of the mind as well as their biological substrate.

Britta Blomberg draws on the treatment of two children with autism in her meticulous study of the development of the concepts of space and time and of the "theory of mind"—concepts she borrows from developmental and cognitive research. Following Alvarez, who emphasized the importance of grammar as a reference point for the development of thought as well as for the technique of interpretation, Blomberg traces parallels between her patients' developing capacity for emotional and linguistic communication.

Julia Pestalozzi refers to the idea of "psychotic functioning in adolescence" proposed by Moses and Eglé Laufer (1984). Adolescents in a state of "psychotic functioning" do not exhibit thought disorder or the collapse of their mental faculties, unlike those suffering from adolescent psychosis in the psychiatric sense. Nor do they turn to hallucinatory "neo-realities" as a refuge from a reality they experience as unbearable. It is their body image that is subject to a profound split: between the pregenital body image of childhood and the sexual body image of adolescence. Pestalozzi emphasizes the concrete thinking that is characteristic of these adolescents, and which tends to take the place of symbolic thinking and to give "the impression of a reality that is tangible, comprehensible and unambiguous". The analysis of Pestalozzi's patient Daniel provides striking illustrations of her argument, which, unlike the Laufers' formulation, does not posit an impermeable barrier between "psychotic functioning" and psychosis proper.

Didier Houzel describes a phenomenon that he considers to be characteristic of autistic organizations: a very early split in the bisexuality of the containing object. He proposes that this containing object is not only maternal, but that it necessarily includes paternal elements deriving from the mother's identification with her own father. In their guise of the nipple, these paternal elements come between the child's hungry mouth and the nourishing breast; they support the maternal container by protecting it from intrusion, and they endow it with the necessary consistency and elasticity. Children with autism appear to have made a very early split between the maternal and paternal elements of the containing object. This primitive split becomes manifest primarily in the countertransference of the therapist, whose task it will be to modify it: in himself (or herself) in the first instance, and then, by means of interpretation, in the child. Such splits may also be observed in what Frances Tustin called "autistic pockets", which are present in many psychopathological constellations in children, adolescents and adults.

Suzanne Maiello discusses Didier Houzel's proposals with regard to her own work on the sound object and on the foetus's pre-natal experience of sound and rhythm. These, together with the action of the uterine environment in counteracting the effect of gravity, provide a containing object. Birth can therefore mean a catastrophic rupture of the containment provided by ongoing rhythms unless this is healed by an emotionally vital relationship with the mother.

Finally, we have particular pleasure in including edited versions of two of the "conversations" with senior clinicians that took place at the Caen conference on Psychosis in Childhood and Adolescence (the others were with Yolanda Gampel, Bianca Lechevalier, and Salomon Resnik). The work of both Geneviève Haag and Raymond Cahn has not so far been widely translated into English: the publication of this volume is therefore a welcome opportunity to present aspects of their highly influential work to an English-speaking audience.

Note

1. Hodges (2004), in a critical review of the major cognitive theories put forward to account for autism, points to the clinical observations that are left unaccounted for by all of these theories. She argues for a developmental theory such as that put forward by Hobson (1993, 2002), which acknowledges the primacy of interpersonal relationships.

Selected Bibliography on Psychosis[1]

Classic references

Bick, E. (1968). The experience of the skin in early object relations. *International Journal of Psycho-analysis*, *49*: 484–486.

Bion, W. R. (1967). *Second Thoughts.* London: Heinemann [reprinted, London: Karnac, 1984].

Cecchi, V. (1990). The analysis of a little girl with an autistic syndrome. *International Journal of Psycho-Analysis, 71*: 403–410.

Klein, M. (1930). The importance of symbol-formation in the development of the ego. In: *The Writings of Melanie Klein, volume 1.* London: Hogarth, 1975.

Klein, M. (1935). A contribution to the psychogenesis of manic-depressive states. In: *The Writings of Melanie Klein, volume 1.* London: Hogarth, 1975.

Klein, M. (1946). Notes on some schizoid mechanisms. In: *The Writings of Melanie Klein, volume 3.* London: Hogarth, 1975.

Klein, M. (1957). Envy and gratitude. In: *The Writings of Melanie Klein, volume 3.* London: Hogarth, 1975.

Klein, S. (1974). Transference and defence in manic states. *International Journal of Psycho-Analysis, 55*: 397–404.

Klein, S. (1980). Autistic phenomena in neurotic patients. *International Journal of Psycho-Analysis, 61*: 395–402.

Mahler, M. (1968). *On Human Symbiosis and the Vicissitudes of Individuation. Vol 1: Infantile Psychosis.* New York: International Universities Press.

Meltzer, D. (1992). *The Claustrum.* Strath Tay, Perthshire: Clunie Press.

Meltzer, D., Bremner, J., Hoxter, S., Weddell, D. & Wittenberg, I. (1975). *Explorations in Autism.* Strath Tay, Perthshire: Clunie Press.

Milner, M. (1969). *The Hands of the Living God.* London: Hogarth.

Rey, H. (1994). *Universals of Psycho-Analysis in the Treatment of Psychotic and Borderline States.* (J. Magagna, Ed.) London: Free Association Books.

Rosenfeld, D. (1984). Hypochondrias, somatic delusion and body scheme in psycho-analytic practice. *International Journal of Psycho-analysis, 65*: 377–388.

Rosenfeld, H. (1965). *Psychotic States.* London: Hogarth.

Rosenfeld, H. (1987). *Impasse and Interpretation.* London: Routledge.

Searles, H. (1965). *Collected Papers on Schizophrenia and Related Subjects.* London: Hogarth [reprinted, London: Karnac, 1986].

Segal, H. (1981). *The Work of Hanna Segal.* New York: Jason Aronson.

Tustin, F. (1972). *Autism and Childhood Psychosis.* London: Hogarth [reprinted, London: Karnac, 1995].

Tustin, F. (1981b). *Autistic States in Children* (2nd revised edn, 1992). London: Routledge.

Tustin, F. (1986). *Autistic Barriers in Neurotic Patients* (2nd revised edn, 1994). London: Karnac.

Tustin, F. (1990). *The Protective Shell in Children and Adults.* London: Karnac.

Winnicott, D. W. (1958). *Through Paediatrics to Psycho-Analysis.* London: Hogarth.

Winnicott, D. W. (1965). *The Maturational Process and the Facilitating Environment.* London: Hogarth.

Current developments

Alvarez, A. (1992). *Live Company: Psychoanalytic Psychotherapy with Autistic, Borderline, Deprived and Abused Children.* London/New York: Routledge.

Alvarez, A., & Reid, S. (Eds.) (1999). *Autism and Personality: Findings from the Tavistock Autism Workshop.* London/New York: Routledge.

Barrows, K. (1999). Ghosts in the swamp: some aspects of splitting and their relationship to parental losses. *International Journal of Psycho-Analysis, 80*: 549–561.

Barrows, P. (2002). Becoming verbal: autism, trauma and playfulness. *Journal of Child Psychotherapy, 28*: 53–72.

Bergman, A. (1999). *Ours, Yours, Mine: Mutuality and the Emergence of the Separate Self.* Northvale, NJ: Jason Aronson.

Haag, G. (1991). Some reflections on body ego development through psychotherapeutic work with an infant. In: R. Szur & S. Miller (Eds.), *Extending Horizons.* London: Karnac.

Haag, G. (1997). Psychosis and autism: schizophrenic, perverse and manic-depressive states during psychotherapy. In: M. Rustin, M. Rhode, A. Dubinsky, & H. Dubinsky (Eds.), *Psychotic States in Children.* London: Duckworth.

Haag, G. (2000). In the footsteps of Frances Tustin: further reflections on the construction of the body ego. *International Journal of Infant Observation, 3*: 7–22.

Houzel, D. (1996). Bisexual aspects of the countertransference in the therapy of psychotic children. In: J. Tsiantis, A.-M. Sandler, D. Anastasopoulos, & B. Martindale (Eds.), *Countertransference in Psychoanalytic Psychotherapy with Children and Adolescents.* EFPP Clinical Monograph Series, London: Karnac.

Houzel, D. (2001). Bisexual qualities of the psychic envelope. In: J. Edwards (Ed.), *Being Alive: Building on the Work of Anne Alvarez.* London: Brunner-Routledge.

Houzel, D. (2001). The "nest of babies" fantasy. *Journal of Child Psychotherapy, 27*: 125–138.

Houzel, D. (2004). The psychoanalysis of infantile autism. *Journal of Child Psychotherapy, 30*: 225–237.

Jackson, M. (2001). *Weathering the Storms: Psychotherapy for Psychosis.* London: Karnac.

Jackson, M., & Williams, P. (1994). *Unimaginable Storms: A Search for Meaning in Psychosis.* London: Karnac.

Lechevalier, B. (1997). Expressions of annihilation anxiety and the birth of the subject. In: T. Mitrani & J. L. Mitrani (Eds.), *Encounters with Autistic States: A Memorial Tribute to Frances Tustin.* Northvale, NJ: Jason Aronson.

Maiello, S. (1995). The sound object: a hypothesis about pre-natal auditory experience and memory. *Journal of Child Psychotherapy, 21*: 23–42.

Maiello, S. (2001). Prenatal trauma and autism. *Journal of Child Psychotherapy, 27*: 107–124.

Resnik, S. (2001). *The Delusional Person.* London: Karnac.

Rhode, M. (2000). On using an alphabet: recombining separable components. In: J. Symington (Ed.), *Imprisoned Pain and its Transformation; a Festschrift for H. Sydney Klein.* London: Karnac.

Rhode, M. (2004). Different responses to trauma in two children with autistic spectrum disorder: the mouth as crossroads of the sense of self. *Journal of Child Psychotherapy, 30*: 3–20.

Rhode, M., & Klauber, T. (Eds.) *The Many Faces of Asperger's Syndrome.* London: Karnac.

Rosenfeld, D. (1992). *The Psychotic Aspects of the Personality.* London: Karnac.

Rustin, M. (1997). Rigidity and stability in a psychotic patient: some thoughts about obstacles to facing reality in psychotherapy. In: M. Rustin, M. Rhode, A. Dubinsky, & H. Dubinsky (Eds.), *Psychotic States in Children.* London: Duckworth.

Rustin, M., Rhode, M., Dubinsky, A., & Dubinsky, H. (Eds.) (1997). *Psychotic States in Children.* London: Duckworth.

Note

1. Only publications in English are referred to; much important work has had to be omitted for reasons of space.

CHAPTER ONE

Autism and psychosis[1]

Anne Alvarez

Philip Roth wrote recently that politics and literature are not only in an inverse relation to each other, they are in an antagonistic relationship:

> To politics, literature is decadent, soft, irrelevant, boring, wrong-headed, dull, something that makes no sense and really oughtn't to be. Why? because the particularizing impulse *is* literature. How can you be an artist and renounce the nuance? But how can you be a politican and allow the nuance? As an artist the nuance is your task. Your task is *not* to simplify. The task remains to impart the nuance, to elucidate the complication, to imply the contradiction. [Roth, 1998, p. 223]

For politician and artist, one could read researcher and clinician, or diagnostician and therapist. Yet the relationship need not be antagonistic. I will be saying a lot about nuances and complexities in children with autism and psychosis, but I shall also make a tiny attempt to bring some order to bear on the clinical issues and on the nature of these mysterious conditions of childhood.

I will begin with a discussion of autism and end with some links with borderline psychosis and personality disorder.

Autism

The question of the primary impairment in autism

There is much controversy about how best to describe autism, about where to locate the core damage, and about the nature of the core impairment. Some authors prefer a cognitive explanation, i.e., that people with autism are born without the capacity eventually to form an adequate "theory of mind" (Frith, 1989; Leslie, 1987). Clinical findings from psychotherapy, together with the study of very early infantile development, which has supported psychoanalytic ideas regarding the social/emotional foundations of cognition—that is, *the precursors of* "the precursors of theory of mind" (Baron-Cohen *et al.*, 1996)—has led us at the Tavistock Autism Workshop (Alvarez & Reid, 1999) to concur with writers like Hobson (1993) and Trevarthen and colleagues (1996) who view autism as a disorder of intersubjectivity, as a lack of a sense of other persons. Hobson (*ibid.*, p. 15) points out [and much developmental research (Stern, 1985) and naturalistic infant observation (Miller, Rustin, Rustin, & Shuttleworth, 1989; Reid, 1997) support his assertion] that the concept of persons is more fundamental than either the concept of bodies or the concept of minds. Susan Reid and I have formulated the autistic impairment as an impairment of the normal *sense of mutual, emotionally-based curiosity about, and desire for, interpersonal relationships*.

We do not suggest that such impairment is the *primary cause* of the disorder. The complexities of multiple causation, and the interaction between genetic, pre-natal, and post-natal environmental factors must await further research. We do suggest, however, that such impairment in relatedness needs to be addressed as the core and primary impairment. Such primary impairment (with its related deficits and disorders) needs to be distinguished from secondary disorders, tertiary deviance, and a fourth factor that accompanies all three, that of the individual child´s personality and motivations. All four factors need our attention during assessment and treatment: their accurate description is relevant, by the way, to the important question of subgroups of autism (Wing & Attwood, 1987; Wing & Gould, 1979). The passive, indifferent, "undrawn" child who has never quite awakened to the interestingness of people and of the world may require a somewhat more active technique from us than does the more aloof and avoidant, "withdrawn", "shell-type" child. The former may need help to become a person, the latter to reveal his hidden personhood. We may need to draw very close to the former, and be careful to respect distances with the latter. Of course, children do not stay put in neat diagnostic categories, and the same child may need a different approach at different moments. Yet, it is worth noting the differences between these varying states of mind, and the patients themselves seem to appreciate our sensitivity to such nuances.

Work with families, schools and the network

The trauma of having one's child receive a diagnosis of autism, and the degree of confusion and rejection experienced by those who live with such a child, have been well documented by Susan Reid (1999) and Trudy Klauber (1999) in *Autism and Personality*. They note, however, that it is not only the anguish and disappointment that needs processing: there is also the further problem of the ways in which families may have come to adapt to their child's condition. They may have begun to give up expecting ordinary parental rewards; they may have settled for a lesser form of relatedness. A pull on the wrist by the child will get the required banana, the grunt tends to get the door opened. Parents may need much help not only to mourn the lost healthy child, but also to rediscover what health remains, and to hold out for it against their child's bad habits of mind. They may need, like therapists and teachers, to learn to read very faint signals of health where larger signs are absent, or to begin to set more ordinary boundaries and to make more ordinary demands for civilized behaviour. I am not going into detail about this work with parents and the network, but wish to say that the work with the individual child, except under very rare conditions, cannot proceed without it. A few examples will emerge when I get to the clinical material.

The work with both child and parents needs to be twin-pronged: it addresses both the autistic symptomatology and the intact or spared "non-autistic" part of the child, however developmentally delayed this may be (see Bion, 1957 on the distinction between psychotic and non-psychotic parts of the personality). These two aspects of the patient's functioning have two widely differing trajectories or courses of development and both need careful study, and treatment where possible. For all its apparent stasis, the autistic condition is much less static and more mutable than it sometimes appears. While a micro-second's glance by a child at a new toy in the room may be followed by an instantaneous return to old rituals, the quality of the child's glance may nevertheless offer a clue, a faint signal that can be amplified and built upon tactfully.

Bion did not discuss the question of the age of the healthy part, but I would stress that it is vital that therapists assess, and, indeed, carers be alert to, the precise developmental level at which this apparently more normal part of the self may be operating. The child's chronological age may be five or ten years, but the non-autistic part may, depending on how long the child has had autism, be very much younger. The "infantile" part of the personality described by Klein and others may be two years, three months, or even three weeks of age. When the child finally becomes interested in toys, or games, say, these may need to be more suitable for a baby of ten months than a child of five years. This information can be usefully exchanged between members of the treatment team and teachers or carers, any one of whom may be the first to note a possible new development or problem. The difficult issue of when a child will not manage a new activity, when he cannot, and when he feels he cannot, is another issue that requires good collaboration, where we all need help from each other to better understand these children. We do not consider our approach as a rival to educational or behavioural interventions, only as a complement. A more manageable or more educated child may produce a somewhat happier child and family, but a more *interested*, psychologically engaged child may bring even more pleasure to himself and others.

I now want to return to the individual treatment, the first premise of which is a psychoanalytic object-relations one. That is, we do not study only the patient's self, but also the state of his internal objects and object relations. These internal figures may need treatment just as much as the self does. Several authors have commented that both in developmental research and in psychoanalysis, the old split between emotion and cognition is breaking down. Urwin (1987) pointed out that we need no longer see emotion as slowing down or speeding up cognition, but as *entering into the structure of cognition itself*. The interestingness of the world is not appreciated on a purely cognitive level and psychoanalysis has much to offer on this subject. The second premise of the therapy is that a disorder of the capacity for social interaction may benefit from a treatment that functions via the process of social interaction itself. The third one asserts, as I have said, that the treatment must take account of the *developmental level at which the child is functioning at any given moment.*

I now want to comment briefly on treatment of deficit or delay, and then spend somewhat more time on issues of disorder and deviance.

Addressing the deficit: therapeutic implications of deficit in the internal object

Waking the child to mindfulness and amplifying preconceptions

This aspect of the work is more relevant to the undrawn, not the withdrawn, child. The child may not yet be interested in us, but he may begin by becoming interested in our interest in him. This particular subgroup of autistic children seems to be rather like Wing's passive indifferent group, and appear to be lost, rather than hiding. Unlike the Rainman, whose brother tells him he knows he's in there, these patients seem to have forgotten, or perhaps have never quite known that they are in there and others are out there. In this state of mind, (because the categories do shift at moments), a more active technique of "reclamation", of calling the child into eye contact, say, may be helpful, (so long as it is tactful and distances are respected if the child becomes avoidant in the next moment).

One three-year-old girl, Angela, had a repetitive preoccupation with doors, and spent the first two assessment sessions staring through the door of a dolls' house. My colleague and I speculated, together with her equally mystified mother, whether it was the tunnel effect that attracted her; was it the symmetry—there was a window opposite—or was it the inside of the house that fascinated her? Nothing seemed to fit. On impulse, in the third session I got down on my knees and peeked back at her through the back window of the house. The effect was electric: Angela was delighted, and celebrated by plunging her head smiling in her mother's lap. I do not think that Angela was *looking for a human face* at that moment. Yet she knew it when she saw it. We underlined Angela's wish to share her pleasure with her mother. There are important issues here: first, it is important, during an assessment, to discover the child's capacity to respond; at the same time, it is equally important to help parents to learn how to engage the child better, without making the parents feel accused of having given up, or of being responsible for the child's original autistic condition. Angela's needs were not being clearly expressed. In this situation the child and parent can fall or drift further and further apart. If Angela was looking for something, she didn't quite know or remember what it was. She was in a state of pre-expectation, rather than expectation. Like Klaus and Kennell's (1982) and Brazelton's (Brazelton, Koslowski, & Main, 1974) mothers calling their babies into contact, I think for a moment I provided what Bion (1962) called a realization of a preconception, not of a concept. I met a pre-need, not a need. The child needs repair to his ego defects (Sandler & Sandler, 1958)) but also to the defects in his internal objects. Everyone concerned with the child may need to be sensitized to respond to, channel, and amplify signals that are weak, delayed, or highly immature. We may find ourselves responding in a manner similar to the mother of a two-week-old baby, and this may begin the repair of faulty internal objects.

It is not only our social and socializing behaviour that needs to be developmentally informed. Our language too, may need to be simple, not to demand too much two-tracked complicated thinking arising from "why–because" interpretations, i.e., "you are angry because . . ." may be too much for a confused, disorientated or unorientated child. Simply getting to know that he is angry today, and finding out what that feels like, may be a vital first step that should not be skipped over. At moments, the therapist may even have to use what Trevarthen has called "motherese", a soft singsong voice—in common parlance, baby talk—to get through to a child who does not listen to ordinary, more adult- or schoolage-appropriate speech.

Play, too, may need to be very simplified. If the child has never played ball, then we may first have to begin with finding out if he has any interest in passing objects from his hand to ours, or even, as with even younger babies, accepting objects from our hand to his. Ball play may be months away if this early stage of turn-taking, and the even earlier stage of proto-conversational turn-taking, has not been reached. At other moments, of course, when the child is more present and aware and his behaviour has more intentionality and motive, more ordinary psychotherapeutic work may take place. I would maintain that the work with these children remains both developmentally and psychoanalytically informed. Getting a balance between, on the one hand, attempts to focus and engage the child, to turn preconceptions into concepts, by being developmentally attuned and therefore more active, and, on the other hand, leaving him space to have his own experience once he is enough *in himself* to be able to do this, is a perpetually difficult task. It is by no means simply a question of playing with the child.

Some possible primary disorders of arousal and introjection

Samuel, a four-year-old patient of mine, was a very tense boy with severe autism and at first he seemed full of a barely controlled, almost frenzied excitement. He had several relentless and repetitive behaviours, gazing at his claw-like fist, or at running water, or at spinning wheels, or his own reflection in shiny surfaces. Some while into treatment, when he was much calmer and more related, I was astonished to find that, even at his most happy, friendly, co-operative, and less autistic moments, his heart was racing like a terrified wild bird's. I never learned whether it was racing in the same way when he was off in a corner absorbed in one of his repetitive behaviours and out of emotional and social reach; I certainly got the impression that sometimes these behaviours did serve to calm him; they were a bizarre and dangerously addictive, but nevertheless effective form of self-soothing.

Psychoanalytic clinicians were among the first to comment on the problem of excitement and excitability in children with autism. Tustin (1981b) described the children's difficulty in "filtering" experience, their states of unbearable ecstasy: she described a child completely overwhelmed by the yellowness of a yellow flower. Meltzer (1976, p. 20) suggested that they were bombarded by stimuli. American researchers have explored what they have called unusual levels of arousal in children with autism (Dawson & Lewy, 1989). This work adds another dimension to the psychology and the psychoanalysis of autism. It reminds us that the positive or negative content of experience is only one aspect; another is its intensity. Many children with autism seem to be as disturbed by positive experiences as by negative. Questions of intensity, overload, oversensitivity and over- and under-stimulation are very much the subject of study in infant development research and infant observation. They relate to the question of how, or for that matter, whether, experience can be taken in or introjected.

To return to the question of how to understand Samuel's racing heart, or what Dawson calls "arousal" and its effects, avoidant behaviour and frustration have been shown to be associated with increase in heart rate but, in infancy, the orientating response and attention to the environment are associated with *decrease* in heart rate (Tronick, 1989). Samuel seemed to want contact with me at such moments—to be orientating towards me and attending to me, not avoiding me—but yet, at the same time, he was very disturbed by it. Dawson and Lewy (1989) stressed the importance of therapies that take into account the question of what is the optimal level of stimulation for a child. Many of these children are thrown into a terribly turbulent universe when they relax their guard. I think this may be more characteristic of what Wing and Attwood (1987) termed the "aloof" subgroup, [or what Tustin (1981b) called the shell-type child] than of the more floppy indifferent child (see previous section and Wing and Attwood, 1987 on the "passive" subgroup).

Disordered arousal and introjection: lowering the intensity

Samuel, like his mother, was very short-sighted, but as he often destroyed his glasses with his ritualistic shaking of them, his mother suggested he leave them with her during the sessions. I was, after all, not teaching him or asking for close work. After about six months' treatment, Samuel, who had hardly ever stopped to look at *anything* in the room, finally became interested in a little blue cube-shaped brick. Much work had to be done in helping him to "filter" even an experience as apparently simple and easy as gazing at a brick. Some weeks later, he noted that there was more than one brick, and began to pick up two identical blue ones at a time. He would look at them briefly, as though for a fleeting second he was examining and enjoying their symmetry and the way he could put the two cubes neatly together, and then he would suddenly squash them together and make them explode into the air, as though they had erupted. He would be overcome by the same sort of disturbing excitement whenever he came close and looked into my eyes or at my face. Then he would suddenly dash away, carry out his hand ritual, and lay his face close to the open section of the window. At first, I thought he had returned to the old autistic state of mind, but I began to suspect that he was often still in touch with me at such moments. I came to think that he had simply gone over to the window to "cool down".

After another six months, he had slowed down somewhat, and could study the shapes of the bricks very closely, build towers, and post some into appropriate holes in shape-sorter toys. I wondered how this had come about, and what might have been the major preconditions. I did not have the impression that the explosions were simply the result of an enraged attack on twoness [as in Bion's (1959) concept of "Attacks on linking"]. Samuel was, I think, having difficulty in coping with excitement, and also with the comprehension that twoness could be available to him *in time*—that there was enough time to look at both bricks, not *precisely* at the same instant. In fact, from the way he first began to look at my face, I got the impression that he had never learned how to scan, which is how most people manage to sustain eye contact. In the beginning, he never met my eyes for more than a peripheral fleeting instant, but when he did, his gaze was too strong, and then he would have to tear his eyes away, just as babies do in the early days of life before they have learned to scan (Stern, 1985). He needed a temporal container that could help him to find out how not to make do with one, but to have two *in sequence*, one at a time. I did not ask the question of myself or his family at the time, but I wonder now whether he had ever played passing an object from one hand to the other, which, as Bruner (1968) has suggested, is important as a reflection of the developing concept of twoness. I heard of a baby in an infant observation who tried this out immediately after a feed when the father had suggested to the mother that the baby could hold her own spoon while the mother fed her with another. First the feeding spoon held by the mother went in his mouth, then the baby's own, in a kind of turn-taking. About ten minutes after the feed was over, the baby began to pass an object carefully from one hand to another: it seemed possible that the baby had been able to take in, and was practising in order to internalize, some idea that two people could have agency, and each could wait while the other had his turn. Bruner suggested that such co-ordinations are based on earlier co-ordinations, e.g., the acts of sucking and of looking in the early days and weeks of life. But co-ordinations of sensory modalities were difficult for Samuel, and patience was foreign to him, too. I had to work hard to slow him down sufficiently to help him to conceive of a universe that could exist comfortably in the dimension of time. (I have wondered whether such early co-ordinations of two positive features of the object—suckable and lookable-at—might be necessary precursors of the more major co-ordinations between positive and negative features of the object in the depressive position.)

Disordered arousal and introjection: tuning in to the right band of intensity

In the later stages of Samuel's treatment, when he had learned to enjoy playing ball with people, there would sometimes come a moment when he would suddenly throw the ball at me very viciously. The ball was large and fairly soft, so there was no danger to me. I began to notice that if I threw it back too gently afterwards, perhaps in an attempt to contain and transform the violent emotions fuelling his throw, he would seem deflated and disappointed. Also, if I became somewhat strict because it had gone near something breakable in the room, he looked persecuted and upset. Yet, if I threw it back as viciously as he had, but in a humorous, slightly dramatized and hammed-up manner, he loved it. In the same way, if—again after some years of treatment—he resorted to his ritualistic hand movement, or teetered dangerously on the edge of a table in his socks, not in the old absorbed autistic way, but in a now provocative and irritating manner, my response had to be very precisely calibrated. I found that if I did not feel irritated or disappointed and simply commented calmly that he was trying to irritate me, he redoubled his efforts. Sometimes—but not always—he may have heard an edge to my voice and sensed the hypocrisy in it. If I asked him to stop in a tone that conveyed too much undigested irritation, he became embittered, and again redoubled his efforts. At such moments, I think he felt I was colluding in a nasty power game. The point I wish to emphasize is that even the non-hypocritical, non-forced, genuinely friendly response on my part could disappoint him profoundly if it was too calm. Yet if I dramatized and hammed up a humorous, warm, but genuine exasperation, in the manner of, "OH NO, NOT THAT BORING HAND AGAIN", he would yelp and roar with laughter and delight, and seem somehow wonderfully invigorated. The bitterness would go out of the situation, and he would often stop his ritual and resume a more open and related type of play. I became certain that if he were to feel really understood and really heard, it was not only a question of my getting the emotional content right, *but also* of reaching the right level of intensity. I am convinced that his powerful vitality required a loud enough or big enough answer.

Greenspan (1997) has very interesting things to say on these therapeutic issues. He makes an important distinction between regulatory "factors" that distinguish one (normal) infant or child from another, and regulatory "disorders". He also says that it is important with hyper-aroused patients naturally to help them to come down, i.e., to down-regulate, but not too much—if you bring them too far down, you may lose their attention and interest.

Daniel Stern (1974) refers to the slowness of tempo and grossness of exaggerations of mothers' behaviour towards their infants. He says this probably matches closely the range of infant preferences and tolerances of rate and degree of stimulus change.

> The slowness of the tempo, along with the exaggeration, may enable the infant to maintain the identity of the mother's face across its various physical transformations and thus facilitate the acquisition of a stable face schema. Normal adult facial expressions flash very rapidly and conceivably could present the infant with a discontinuous sequence of faces. [Stern, 1974, p. 192]

I do not have the impression that Samuel was likely to have been particularly rushed by his caregivers in early infancy: I can imagine, however, that he had an intolerance—that he himself was simply unable to slow down and quieten enough as a baby to use what was available to him. I often felt that my room was too small, my voice too thin, the world too puny for his vast but enormously *compressed* vitality.

Oliver Sacks (1995) has described the problems of Virgil, the fifty-year-old Olkahoman, blind since the age of five, who had his vision restored forty-five years later. At first, he had no appreciation of depth or distance. Street lights were luminous stains stuck on window panes and the corridors of the hospital were black holes. Moving objects, such as his cat at home, or a human faces greeting him with mobile features, were impossible. He could manage the details of the cat—tail, back, head; he was used to taking it in sequentially by touch—but could not grasp *movement at a glance*. I suspect that Samuel's years of gaze-avoidance and his extreme myopia may have made him a bit like Virgil. When he did start to want to look at the world, he wanted desperately to see everything in one glance. Gradually, something began to change and his eye contact became more sustained. His vision improved, and, incidentally, I heard that his glasses' prescription had approached the normal. I guessed that he was finally using his eye muscles. I had indeed often slowed my face and speech down when he began to explore objects, and, because he hated being interfered with, one had to pace one's interventions very carefully. Even so, his new curiosity cost him dear, and he began to look exhausted half way through a session.

Concepts of defence and regulation

Earlier, I stressed the importance of approaching autism, for purposes both of description and treatment, from a psychoanalytic object-relations perspective, that is, via a two-person psychology, involving a close study of the patient's internal object representations and relationships. I also emphasized the need for the therapist to tune her responses to the appropriate developmental level. As I became ever more awed by some of these patients' wild swings in levels of arousal and excitement, I have also come to think that the developmentalists' concept of "regulation" provides an essential supplement to the more usual psychoanalytic concept of defence. Defences are meant to stop someone having an experience (or at least feeling it) whereas a regulatory function may allow the experience and the feeling through, but under bearable yet sufficiently demanding and interesting conditions. Regulation may thereby assist important introjective processes. The question of who—the self, the internal object, or an external figure—does the regulating is another matter (see Tronick, 1989).

Addressing both disorder and developmental delay together

Sometimes the therapist may need to hold out strongly for non-autistic, non-ritualistic ways of calming down. Subsequent to the early period of Samuel's rejection of me, there came a period when he would seek my lap as a place of refuge from his agitations or frustrations, and even make a lot of very close eye contact while he was there. He was, however, a very sensual child, and as time progressed I began to feel that, as he was now sufficiently interested in face-to-face contact to be willing to accept it from a few feet instead of a few inches, he should be able to begin to use a small chair that I drew up next to mine. It took about six months to persuade him to use it! He felt rejected at first, and, as so many of these children do, tended to retreat to autism. I found I had to function as a sort of traffic policeman: on the one hand, stopping his physical intrusions; on the other, beckoning him *at the same instant* to the chair, while my voice suggested that we could have a "talk". He had begun by then to engage in and to enjoy playful proto-conversation, but he seemed to have no idea that he could do the same thing at a slight distance. (Normal babies learn to extend the distance at which they can make face-to-face contact in the early months of life (Papousek & Papousek, 1975).) In a way, by beginning to refuse to offer my lap, I was addressing an activity that was in the process of becoming a disorder, with the accompanying danger of leading on to more deviant behaviour (and tertiary disorder?). By deviant, I mean that the normal infant's desire for the caregiver's lap can, in the autistic child, become solidified and embedded into something that may, in these often highly sensual children, become intrusive and antisocial. It can also become antidevelopment and stand in the way of other important achievements, such as speech. In offering the chair and the "talk", I was addressing the deficit or developmental delay in his understanding that more distant contact was still contact of a kind and pleasurable. In other words, I was introducing the concept that frustration need not imply that alternative forms of living were unavailable. I do not mean to imply that frustration on its own was not important also for Samuel's development, nor that I saw my task as a placation of his intolerance. I mean that at some moments, when his desperation and despair were very great and when he could not conceive of survival without recourse to autism, then I had to ensure that he understood that there was an alternative.

Repetitive behaviours

I have mentioned moments when Samuel seemed to be using his repetitive behaviours for self-soothing, or even in a far more normal manner, to irritate another person. But repetitive behaviours are not simply linked with disorders of regulation. There are personal motives for, and consequences of, such activities. Can psychotherapists' felt perceptions in the countertransference, when we *sit for long enough* with such children, teach us anything about the rituals? Deficit requires repair, but what do we do about disorder? And what if something more than disorder is involved? The problem is that, as the child grows older, these "bad habits" become more and more ingrained, more and more a way of life, and may contribute to autism as a chronic condition. The chronicity can make the child even more unreachable, partly because normal development is interfered with by the persistence of this symptom, but partly also because the rituals gather to themselves more and more motivations, both developmental and antidevelopmental, sometimes even deviant.

Deviance

Tustin's (1981a) concept of the autistic "object" was a revelation to psychoanalytic clinicians trying to find meaning in the repetitive rituals of their autistic patients. She showed that such objects were not full of symbolic meanings relating to live human figures: rather they were used *instead* of such figures to shut meaning and life out. It is interesting how much is implied in Kanner's (1943) description of rituals as the result of an "anxiously obsessive desire for sameness". At some moments, the rituals may indeed be carried out anxiously; at others, they are carried out in a rather lazy, comfortable, even complacent manner; and sometimes they seem quite desultory, not even comforting. The ritual goes on, although there seems to be no obvious motivation for it at all. The child is stuck.

My experience with an earlier patient, Robbie, suggested that a particular repetitive preoccupation could begin as a way of managing some state of disturbance or of emptiness, or, sometime later in his treatment, even as an object of genuinely fresh interest. But the fuel that afterwards kept it going was neither the disturbance nor the emptiness nor the novel interest. It was something else. Like bronze, the rituals had a way of keeping their shape even after the cast was removed. Once the mould is cast, the binding agents may be of a different order altogether and not amenable to being analysed away by simple explanatory interpretations referring to whatever causal agent may have first set the activity in motion. The repetitive activities at times act like a drug—they have a terrible pull and power. I had to remember not to use particular words that could push Robbie over into the gluey mental world of his ritualistic talk. It was like walking on marshy ground: I had to try to keep to the tussocks. If I slipped, we were both lost in the swamp. His rituals had a pull like the power of the force of gravity, or like huge suckers. I had to confront this force *before it took hold,* because lazy desultoriness and stickiness could easily and rapidly move on to strange excitements.

Strange excitements as a consequence of repetitive behaviours: tertiary autism?

I have mentioned the particular importance of the use of feelings aroused in the countertransference in understanding these children. There is a further reason why an emotive clinician's language is needed to give an accurate description. It has to do with the clinician's perceptions of the qualitative nature of the rituals themselves at certain moments: that is, the perception of some disturbing qualities that occasionally become attached to the rituals. There are times when abnormal excitements, thrills, frenzies, and even sexual arousal may attach themselves to the rituals and may play a large part in their perpetuation. It is important to remember that a young person with autism, who has little connection to the outside world of human relationships, may be hit particularly hard, for example, by the arrival of puberty and of greater sexual feeling. He may feel rather like a car with an engine revving frantically but with no clutch to transmit the power to the wheels and so move it forward. What happens, then, to the torrent of sexual feeling? The ordinary outlets of interpersonal relations, and the usual adolescent peer group flirtations, gossip, and sexual experimentation are unavailable. It seems as though a river of energy and feeling is dammed up, and must turn on itself in whirlpools, eddies, and strange currents, and even, in places, spread too far afield, where it rests eventually in stagnant pools.

Kanner (1943) referred to the fact that certain actions and rhythmic movements were accompanied by an ecstatic fervour that strongly indicated the presence of masturbatory gratification, but this observation has, to my knowledge, never appeared again in the psychiatric literature on autism. Psychoanalysts like Tustin (1981b) and Meltzer (1975b, pp. 25–26) did comment on the fetishistic quality of the play with some toys or objects. Robbie, in anxious moments, could lick the inside of his lower lip apparently for purposes of self-soothing; but at other times he gave himself over to it, he licked it with a highly sensual pleasure, and the expression on his face at such moments was unpleasantly lascivious and somehow triumphant.

The understanding of idiosyncratic sexual acts, or fantasies with idiosyncratic sexual content, has a long history in psychoanalysis. The understanding, however, that such fantasies may express themselves more indirectly, not through the content but through the *form of verbal presentation* is a somewhat more recent formulation. Joseph (1982) called it "chuntering". She was discussing adult borderline psychotic patients, but her work also applied to other sorts of patients: she showed the strange states of excitement some of her patients got into when they appeared simply to be talking about their depression and misery. Other features and phantasies, however, revealed that their repetitive complaining conversations, especially if they could get her to join in, were producing excitement, even sexual excitement, for them. I had to learn to become very alert to the way Robbie's repetitive, apparently anxious and concerned conversations could so easily go over into states of high sexual excitement, especially if I was too slow to see the warning signs.

Personality: normal, disordered and deviant

I suggested earlier that it may be useful to distinguish between primary and secondary autism. Primary autism may involve original or very early sensitivities or deficits; secondary autism may refer to the symptoms and behaviours that the child develops to cope with his sensitivities or deficits. Both may be tractable to treatment. The secondary autism, however, seems to be particularly influenced by factors in the child's personality, especially the balance between the strength of the intact, non-autistic part, as opposed to the autistic part of the personality. People with autism are more than a collection of symptoms—they are always mysterious, often fascinating, and certainly challenging. But each has his or her own unique personality, needs, preferences, will, and demands, and these deserve as much study as the symptoms themselves. Indeed they often amplify and colour the symptoms. The floppy, passive, autistic child may be as he is partly for constitutional or other reasons, but he may sometimes use his natural passivity or apathy for other more ordinary motives. As a teacher of one of these children said of one very passive child, "Sometimes he is very knowing." The aloof child with his jaw or shoulder set against contact may find contact difficult and unbearable—again for mysterious reason—but anger, disappointment, and despair may feed these reactions against psychologically life-giving social engagement. Strength of character and will can feed the symptoms, but it can also change sides and work on the side of normal engagement with the real world.

The interactions between illness and personality are not always easy to sort out. Some children seem to be autistic out of a helplessness that they cannot change without assistance; others seem to prefer their autism because they dislike the alternative; others seem, quite simply, to be happy in their autism and be all too comfortably ensconced in it. Samuel's impatience, excitement, and difficulty in staying with an interesting (for him) new activity, may have been in part genetic. However, he also seemed to feel that he really *should not have to wait*. On the first occasion when his mother refused to allow him to bring crisps into his session with me, he backed away across the waiting room not in anger, but in *utter disbelief*. He also paid a great deal more visual attention both to her and to me on that occasion than ever before, when crisps had ruled! Such episodes raise the question of character and will as well as of personality.

Behaviour disorder in autism: are there sometimes elements of personality disorder?

Demanding, greedy behaviour, resistance to discipline, to toileting, wild running away, climbing, sexualized intrusiveness—all such behaviours may lead, in some children, to ever greater disorder and eventual deviance as the years go by; the processes of development may become even more skewed. In a small group of children there is sometimes a certain sort of chilling quality in their gaze: unlike those who appear to see *through* people, these regard other people with a clear but cold eye. Such people may, through treatment, give up the worst of their autistic symptoms, but character problems in the form of a sometimes extreme lack of warmth, or of demanding and intrusive behaviour, may remain. Major alterations in character formation may require many years of treatment, difficult but not impossible to provide in the National Health Service. It is very much worth the effort where it can reduce heavy pressures on families and carers, and help the patients themselves to learn to become more friendly and to feel more likeable. They begin to feel that they can win attention, affection, and liking through less forceful methods. Left untreated, features of personality disorder and character formation can be very worrying in adulthood—another argument for the importance of early interventions that take account of the whole of the person with autism.

Barbara

I now want to talk about Barbara, who was referred at age thirteen with a diagnosis by a neuropsychologist of Asperger's Syndrome. Our assessment suggested, however, that there were additional features, both of a borderline condition and of a personality disorder, both of which were deemed amenable to treatment.

Barbara's parents had brought the family to England to get help for her. She was terrified of most animals, of flying on planes, and she was afraid of running or even moving quickly (Rey, 1979). Her sufferings were clearly terrible, but her rigidities, and her excessively demanding and relentlessly repetitive questions, were making her parents' life and their younger daughter's life a misery and at times a torture. They were worried about Barbara's weird muttering—sometimes it was very private; at other times comments concerning the fate that should befall her sister were meant to be heard. Barbara seemed often to be lost in her own world, but when she emerged, she could sometimes take a cold pleasure and pride in some of her cruellest acts—roaring with grim laughter over the memory, for example, of throwing another child's beloved toy down a toilet.

She had been born with chronic diarrhoea, which lasted for the whole of her first three months. She then became a happy, healthy baby and toddler, adored and idealized by all four of her grandparents. She was still not toilet trained when she was sent to a nursery at the age of three, but there, too, she was considered a charming "little princess" and all seemed well. She changed at that point to another nursery school, which turned out to have a very different and extremely rigid regime. They demanded that she should be toilet trained and obedient, and her fall from grace was sudden and absolute. She began holding her faeces, became withdrawn at the school, and their experts went on to suggest, first schizophrenia, then autism. A psychologist disagreed, and I have seen her video of Barbara at home at that time, looking quite normally engaged in play and with her family.

By the time of the first of a series of assessment consultations when she was thirteen years old, Barbara's behaviour was odd indeed. She barely looked at me in the waiting room, simply continued staring at the fishtank. She said, infinitely slowly and icily,

"Wha–a–t . . . a–a–are . . . fishhhhh . . . fo–o–or?" Her walk to the room was as infinitely slow and drawn out. Later, as her parents and I talked, she asked, in the same voice, "Why was my sis–ss–tt–terrrr born?" Her unblinking stare at times was very bold, and at others showed a little interest, though of a rather cool clinical kind. Barbara chose to draw. What she drew was a cow, but one with all its orifices open and all the tubes connecting them exposed.[2] There seemed to be no concept of a valve or sphincter function (Bremner & Meltzer, 1975), and I wonder if she had, somewhere in the part of her that started life with no control of her excretory processes, felt valveless, too. She certainly seemed to have no means of processing and regulating ordinary feelings, even positive ones, when they did flow through her.

A few sessions into the assessment, I had begun to comment to Barbara, humorously but a bit firmly, on the fact that she sometimes really enjoyed keeping the listener waiting for her—with her agonizingly slow speech—to get to the end of the sentence, or making a walking companion slow his pace radically in order to stay near her. She seemed to appreciate my knowing this, and there was a moment of warm eye contact between us: she laughed weakly as though she had been slightly moved. Abruptly she asked, "Why do human beings have two noses?" Her first language is not English, and it took me a moment to realize she meant nostrils. Her communications almost always took the form of questions such as, "Why does gravity have to pull us down?" "Why does time have to go forward?", and so on. Although there were often deep and at times desperate meanings in these questions, she also could use them to control people and to get them to give exactly the kind of educational answer she had come to expect. And sometimes there seemed to be something even more unpleasant in them. But this one about noses fooled me for a moment, until I suddenly realized that she was looking straight into and up my nostrils, and probably, in one sense, right through me. It was an unpleasant and rather chilling experience, particularly because it had followed so quickly on the heels of some real feeling between us. A bit of human contact was followed instantaneously by something that was neither desperate nor simply controlling, but which felt more tertiary and deviant: there was a cold pleasure in it. (This is not to forget that the preoccupation with orifices and their valves had probably begun as a panicky attempt to understand her own shaky start as a baby born with chronic diarrhoea. It is what it had evolved into which is the issue.)

I did a very long consultation/assessment, which continued for a year, partly because no one had a vacancy to take her on. She often spent long periods drawing the anatomy of the eye in perfect detail. We were working hard with her devoted and worried parents to set some boundaries, to help them to stop playing in with answering her controlling but really dead-end questions. We all had to learn to observe some of the deeper and more ordinary human meaning behind them, and to help Barbara to find different ways of getting her emotional needs and anxieties dealt with. I could see that she was at times genuinely terrified to move quickly, but it was clear that at others she used this in a very controlling manner to make companions wait for her in an ever more frustrated state. Her parents were helping her to get a move on into life, and I was encouraging her to walk a little faster; I was also letting her know I knew she enjoyed making the listener wait for her: as I said, she seemed to appreciate the fact I knew this, and agreed with me. I felt she respected me a little when I was firm about the fact that she could easily get a move on if she wanted, although I also needed to show that I understood how terrified she was of losing control and returning to a valveless state. There was a terrible longing for her early "perfect" life that seemed to be hidden in the relentless questions, and her despair was real. These were not always easy balances for me to strike.

One day, after about a year of interrupted twice weekly consultation sessions, I saw a different side of her. She made me wait in the waiting room, at first not looking at me, and then looked at me knowingly. I urged her to come on and she got up saying in her rather booming voice, "The brain . . . knowsss ev–er–y–thinggg . . .". In the consulting room she began to draw an anatomical picture of the ear, showing how sound gets into the brain. I pointed out that she insisted on feeling that her brain knew everything, and it was so hard to acknowledge that she didn't know things—for example, the exact moment when I would come round the door of the waiting room. She had her back turned to me, but she did say a quiet "yes" to this. (At an earlier stage of the work, on occasions when I felt she was more desperate and had no other means of dealing with anxiety, I would not have "disarmed" her in this way, in the sense of removing her defences and stressing the anxiety about not being omniscient. But by now I felt she was stronger, and a bit more grounded. In any case, her defences were not simple defences against anxiety; she was no longer so anxious with me. That is, they were not just symptoms of secondary disorder, in terms of being a means of coping with anxiety. They were also functioning at a tertiary level: she often got a cruel kick out of feeling in control and superior, and seeing other people's discomfiture or concern. Of course, when separations or changes were around, she would revert to using the behaviours in much more needy and desperate ways.)

After her acknowledgement, she started humming a tune which sounded like a folk tune from her home country—solemn, but harmonious, and started drawing how music goes into the brain. "The ear hears the music, and then the brain hears the music," she said, as she drew in every tiny component of its progression on the way through the brain. I decided to challenge this—she was humming still, and even beginning to improvise a bit as I commented on the lovely music. I said that it wasn't really true that her ear heard the music—it was *she* who heard the music, and that although she tried to get control of what happened to her when she heard something or saw something, it didn't happen slowly like in her pictures and speech, it happened very quickly. She began to seem interested. I said things happened to surprise her, and they happened quickly, not slowly. I said I thought she was singing because she was glad to be here again, and that was a surprise and it was quite a nice feeling and why did she so hate surprises? She gradually improvised more in her humming. (I think I was being quite firm with a rigid and extremely powerful side of her, but also noted her problem in handling and regulating the introjection of a pleasant experience. It is possible to speculate that her early lack of a solid inside self may have led to her excessive panic about any kind of free flow inside her, even when it was caused by something as harmless as a feeling.The second trauma of the change from the loving indulgent family situation and nursery to the highly rigid and severe one, may have also have added to her fear and hatred of loss of control. I think on some deep level she felt she lacked regulatory valves and filters in her mind, as well as her body.)

I also commented on her turned back, and she agreed that she liked making me wait endlessly for her attention. She turned more toward me and began looking at me in an interested, almost friendly way—at least, her gaze was less clinical, and I think she may have appreciated the fact I could tolerate waiting for her, even if she couldn't tolerate waiting for me. I saw her suddenly glance over my shoulder up at the toy shelves, and I asked what she was looking at. To my astonishment—she was, after all, fourteen years old and often pretty icy—she whispered, "baby". I brought the baby doll down and she clutched it to herself, patting it with a mixture of urgent fondness and confusion, half-laughing in her excitement and agitation. At first she spanked her and said, "She's got a sore bottom", with the same mixture of agitation and tenderness as before. She indicated that I should speak for the doll, and I started to pretend to cry and to protest that my bottom hurt, and she seemed delighted by that. Then she turned the doll round to face her, and began to stroke her head very tenderly. I spoke for the doll again, and said I liked it when Barbara was kind to me. These moments of tenderness continued to alternate with her picking and poking at the doll's mouth and eyes, with me protesting on the baby's behalf and Barbara laughing helplessly. The laughter seemed partly to do with excited aggression, but also something to do with relief, and real feeling flowing. At moments she was on the edge of tears, and I felt very moved too. It was very different from her usual icy control and her slow tortured sentences.

In spite of the severe personality problems, Barbara's obvious capacity for more ordinary contact with others and with herself made me hopeful that treatment was feasible, and soon after, a therapist with a vacancy was found. The therapist had to work even harder with the borderline aspects of Barbara's condition—on rare occasions, early on, she might have been hallucinating—and Barbara's suffering about what she saw as the finality and irreparability of her plight was intense. The therapist also had to grasp and bridge the two extremely diverse sides of Barbara's personality: the deviant preoccupations were by now very fixed, and yet her capacity for tenderness was profound.

The family and we saw marked improvements in Barbara's capacity to show more openly her humanity. Her gaze was much softened, though still very serious, and she became, after two and a half years' treatment with her therapist (and continuing liaison with her parents and with her excellent school) much more manageable and likeable at home. She herself was gradually able to take more ordinary pleasure in life.

Summary

I have tried to distinguish four factors, deficit or delay, disorder, deviance, and personality. All four features need attention in the treatment of the child or adolescent with autism, psychosis, or personality disorder. Both the autistic and non-autistic, or the psychotic and non-psychotic part of the personality need addressing.

Note

1. The editors wish to thank Taylor & Francis and Karnac for permission to reprint some of this material,which was previously published in Alvarez, 1999 and Alvarez, 2004.
2. See the discussion (Rosenfeld, 1984; Tustin, 1986) of the body as a system of pipes.

CHAPTER TWO

Time, space, and the mind: psychotherapy with children with autism

Britta Blomberg

Mind

When meeting children with autism in psychoanalytically based psychotherapy, it is necessary to have a multi-dimensional approach, in which the growth of the child's cognition presupposes *emotional learning and experience in a social context*. In order to illustrate what psychotherapy with children with autism may entail, I intend to embark from the, nowadays generally accepted, concept of "Theory of Mind". In *Cassell's Concise Dictionary* (1995) "mind" is described as:

> the intellectual powers in man; the understanding, the intellect; the soul; intellectual capacity; recollection, memory; one's candid opinion; sanity; disposition, liking, way of feeling or thinking; intention, purpose; desire, inclination.

"Theory" is described in the same dictionary as:

> supposition explaining something, esp. a generalization explaining phenomena as the results of assumed natural causes; a speculative idea of something, mere hypotheses, speculation, abstract knowledge . . .

I want to start from the concept of mind and argue that *no theory* about this concept can exist before a mind has yet been established. A great deal of literature has been published in recent years on psychoanalytically based psychotherapy with children with autism. Many authors regard the central issue to be a communication disturbance (Alvarez & Reid, 1999, De Astis, 1997, Rhode, 2000). By this perspective one avoids becoming enmeshed in the inflamed debate about the right of interpretation regarding the understanding of the cause of autism. The children, regardless of the cause of their handicap, exhibit severe communication disturbances both towards their closest family and in other relations.

"Nature and nurture"

Experiences are not only something that we are genetically equipped to perceive. The Swedish notions of heredity/environment are very limited in this respect. The English terms "nature" and "nurture" show more clearly the differences between the concepts. While nature is linked to the genetic equipment, nurture represents a *much more active* contribution than the Swedish word "environment". This active component is the very thing with which parents and others important to the child, caregivers and fosterers, for instance, can assist. To quote from Cassell's dictionary again, the following is found regarding the word nurture: "the act of bringing up, training, fostering; nourishment; education; breeding".

Parents, teachers, and therapists of children with autism have to take into account both "nature" and "nurture". Daniel Stern describes infants as competent (1985). They are by *nature* normally equipped (normal perception and the ability to interpret what is perceived). Furthermore, they have parents who are able to provide care, fostering, physical and psychological nearness, a "good-enough mothering" as Winnicott (1965) has described it. There is also a need for a "facilitating environment" (Winnicott, 1965), an external container around the infant and the parents, composed of relatives, friends, work, reasonable housing conditions, etc.

For children with autism, there has been a breakdown in co-operation between these three basic constituents, resulting in things not going well during the child's formative years.

As to *nature*, one must take into account the condition of the child's physical equipment. There are different opinions about the causes of the deficiencies in the "equipment". It is probable that constitutional aspects, as well as early physical traumas in the womb, metabolism anomalies, reactions to vaccine (e.g., mumps, measles, German measles) can affect a child's ability to perceive, register, and systematize impressions. I have worked with children who, in their *nature*, have deficiencies in their capacity do these things. My therapeutic approach must, of course, be influenced by the child's resources. Techniques that make it easier for the child to register and systematize impressions are given a central role. Concepts such as meaning, predictability, and links become recurring themes in my interventions with the child as well as with the parents.

Other children may have "sound equipment", but have endured severe traumas from their experience of "good-enough mothering". It may be a matter of children with traumatic experiences during their first months of life. Children who have been exposed to repeated trauma in their early childhood are unable to *think about* or *process*; they are, of course, far too small to do so and the trauma may be too overwhelming. The link between experiences and emotion has never been established, so what the child has experienced in its body needs to find a place in the therapy room. The therapy often entails a recreating—a "reverie" (Bion, 1962b)—in which the child, with the help of the therapist, can begin to think about continuity in its life. This work rarely commences on a verbal plane but rather, at best, in terms of symbolic representations in the play material. Most frequently, however, it begins with purely physical reactions and attitudes in a tentative interplay with the therapist.

In considering *nurture* and the *facilitating environment*, I have drawn on my many years' experience within the field of child and adolescent psychiatry, in schools and for social services. In such work one comes into contact with children who, unfortunately, are, or have been, maltreated. The adults who should have provided them with nourishment and fostering have failed in their care. We encounter children who, early in life, have not only been subjected to neglect and poor care but also to active physical and psychological abuse (O'Connor & Rutter, 2000).

Sometimes we also meet children with other kinds of deficiencies in *the facilitating environment*. I am thinking here of, for example, premature children who have to struggle in order to survive physically. Physical experiences (representations) of the struggle for survival may remain throughout their lives. They have been subjected to life-giving treatment, but this unfortunately includes essential violations and examinations that hurt such a little body and that the brain does not have a chance to register, systematize, and find out *where* it hurts and *where* the danger is coming from. My therapeutic approach towards a child with this background is affected by my experience of the child having perceived something extremely terrifying. Very often there has not been any other living person present who has been able to contain and share the experience at the time it occurred. Even if parents have been there, it is the still the child itself that has had to endure the physical pain. The environment has, in this way, not been able to be facilitating, but rather the opposite, i.e., perceived as terrifying by the child. Many children with early physical experiences of pain have, despite "good-enough mothering", a deeply-rooted experience in the internal world that mothers and fathers are not to be trusted, as they have not been able to protect them from the unending pain and terror. Containing of psychological pain is of great importance in psychotherapy, as is beginning to find representations of the "nameless dread" that the child bears. The terror is so all-embracing that it cannot be localized to the surrounding world and assume the form of an external enemy. The threat is omnipresent, both within and outside the child.

In other cases it is a matter of physically well-functioning children and parents who are well-functioning in, for example, working life, but who experience great difficulties in thinking about their child's inner world. They find it difficult to discern the child's needs and to interpret (project) their own experiences into the child. They try to read the child's behaviour, but are not able to give meaning to the child's psychological experience.

Some mothers are depressed and although their new-born children may be afforded good external care, the capacity to arouse the child, to be enthusiastic in reasonable doses, is minimal. André Green has written about the enormous difficulties entailed in mourning for a physically present mother, but one who is at the same time psychologically absent (Green, 1993).

Into/inside

One of he first experiences of *inside* that a new-born child perceives is the nipple or the teat of the bottle entering the mouth. In some of the children I have met with the diagnosis autism there have, for various reasons, been problems in this early, physical experience of nursing between mother and child.

The breast, or the teat of the bottle, is the first opportunity the child has of regulating distance: inside its mouth, resting from sucking, with the breast/teat in its mouth or feeling it on its lips and knowing that there is food. The child itself is able to postpone satisfaction, perhaps by looking and smiling at mummy, or to rest his eyes on some object in the room, and then resume the sucking. This regulating of inside–outside, nearness–distance, here–there is a physical precursor to the child, later on in life, to perceive distance and three-dimensionality. This, in turn, leads to the child being able to develop more abstract concepts such as perspective and the capacity to *think about* phenomena from various viewpoints.

Often the deficiencies in the communication capacity of the child with autism is emphasized, and verbal deficiencies in concept formation are stressed. I wish to show how *the whole apparatus of cognitive and emotional concepts* is involved in the problem.

Viktor was three years old when he came to see me. The parents had lived together for a short period when Viktor was born, but were now separated and he lived with his mother, meeting his daddy only occasionally. He had started attending a day nursery when he was eighteen months old, which resulted in "sheer catastrophe" according to his mother. He was not allowed to continue there, and his mother chose to stay at home again for a short period. He began at another day nursery, at which the acclimatization period was very long. He often kept close to the walls and talked to himself. When something went wrong "he went to pieces".

We began psychotherapy with the idea that the mother should go into the room of the parental psychotherapist (once a week) and Viktor into mine (twice weekly). For Viktor and his mother this was far too difficult. The mother "also went to pieces" when she came with him to the one session per week when she did not have anyone to talk to. Eventually we decided that I should take mother and child together into the child therapy room. The mother continued her contact with the parental psychotherapist at another time during the week. The mother and child were extremely close, but the most important thing became not to try to ascertain the aetiology, what the child's behaviour might be due to, but where the behaviour led in the interplay with those in its closest surroundings (Houzel, 2000).

One, two, and three dimensionality

In the beginning, Viktor was completely in his own world. He was a child whom Tustin (1991) describes as entangled or fused. He was not only *one* with his mother, he was *one with everything*. He placed the high-rise buildings in the sand-tray tightly alongside each other, so that the view from the windows was blotted out. He put the cars with their boots up against the next car's bonnet. He let them drive round and round without beginning or end hooked to each other, as if he just had to eliminate any notion of space between the objects. During one session he pulled up a chair for each of us, gave me a fishing rod with a magnet on it (from the fishing game), took the other one for himself and tipped out all the fish into the sand-tray. He insisted on having water in the tray; he couldn't make use of any kind of pretend play. There we sat, side by side, and "fished" and for a fraction of a second he succeeded in making me feel that if we only waited long enough then the paper fish would really bite!

During the therapy sessions we did not have any contact, as I perceived it. As soon as I attempted to make a comment, especially if it was supportive or confirming, he shouted, "Quiet!" (He couldn't even address me with the more imperative "shut up".) The first step for me was that Viktor should be able to experience me as a "facilitating environment". It became important not to be too united with him. What other children perceive as being understood meant for Viktor that I became one, fused, with him. I had to keep to my corner and cautiously comment upon what I saw. I avoided all words that had to do with *you* and *I*. I commented on the series of events in which his characters were involved. When the cars just drove round and round, I could say, "They must be very dizzy . . ."; "How difficult it is to see when one drives so fast . . .". It would have been impossible for me, during this early phase, to connect to any reality between us. There was quite simply no "between us". Everything just *was*. Very often he engaged in incomprehensible harangues, taken from children's books or video films. There was absolutely no way in for me when he was occupied with these. Viktor was probably a quick-witted, alert boy, but he took in far too much of the world. He became totally invaded and had no technique for warding off input and impressions and certainly no space for mutual meetings.

The concept of dimension, such as to *go into/out of* the room and to physically feel concepts such as *foreground/background* became central themes for a long time. What was the corridor and what was the inside of my room? Was one special toy car (foreground) more important than all the others (background)? These concepts are the basis for the capacity to be able to discriminate, systematize, and concentrate, and later on to develop serial sequences.

Concept of time, tense

To actively work with the knowledge of how we use our grammar has been of assistance to me in my therapeutic work. That a child begins to understand concepts such as inside–outside makes it possible for a rudimentary experience of distance, a spatial perception, to exist. This in turn makes it possible to grasp that concepts such as *inside = this, in front of,* and *foreground*. In the same way it is possible to understand the opposite, *outside = that, behind,* and *background*. It is when this physical experience exists that the child, in its mind, is first able to begin to understand what we consider to be self-evident concepts such as, for example, to systematize impressions (Alvarez, 1998). The majority of parents actively assist their child to concentrate by *sharing* the experience of what the child is seeing, e.g., the lamp, as something more important (a foreground) than the ceiling, shadows, and suchlike (background). Through this shared experience the surrounding world is endowed with a *meaning* for the child in a continuous interplay between parents and child. Those children with autism with whom I have worked have all had difficulties in distinguishing *what is essential* and perceiving the rest as background. The capacity to be able to systematize is a prerequisite for the child to be able to think in *sequences*, that is to say, that something comes before something else.

Children like Viktor live entirely in a unbroken *present tense.* If we attempt to imagine this we find ourselves in the same condition as a very young infant or as a severely demented adult. There is no distance, everything just *is.* For Viktor this implied that his cars were simply unable to move forward, they just circled around. They had power, but were unable to move themselves *outwards, forward.* I had to help him very actively to show him the possibility that they would perhaps be able to get to a certain place in the sand-tray. I had to engage in the slow, cautious job of "making the thought thinkable" (Bion, 1962b) long before it could be translated into action. My understanding was that he needed to *feel* and *explore,* with his entire body and all of his mind, the movement forwards and backwards. If, out of therapeutic ambition, I had made the link to reality too prematurely, he would probably have taken in everything I had said, but would not have been able to hold on to anything that had been said.

Anne Alvarez (1992) describes interplay between people in the form of: "catch–hold on to–throw back–receive." Viktor "caught", took in, everything. In his brain all the impressions that he was unable to absorb or systematize created chaos. His only chance was to "throw back", before my words had come inside him, by saying: "Quiet!" Further on in the therapy he was able to say, "I cannot think when you are talking". It became apparent to both of us that he had real difficulty in being able to hold on to something. I had to continue cautiously in my attempts at contacting him. Afterwards it became possible for Viktor to be with me in the room and to take my comments without me destroying his world of ideas, his mind, and therewith himself. He was able to understand that he had an "inside life" (Waddell, 1998), an inner world, which he could have in peace. My comments could not destroy this. My inner world, my thoughts, began much later on to interest him.

During this period of time his mother entered the therapy room. Viktor was developing slowly, but his mother had been outside this enterprise. She very often phoned me saying Viktor was ill or that he didn't want to come and she cancelled the sessions. This was one of the reasons why I considered it necessary to invite Viktor's mother to joint sessions. He was ready (with his dolls and figures) to embark on various adventures—his mother was not. I had to actively "keep mummy company" when Viktor's characters embarked on expeditions of exploration in the sand-tray. His mother and I found an "island" in the sand, where we drank cappuccino (pretend), while maintaining contact with Viktor's characters via messages in toys like bottles and a little telephone. I had to actively introduce the concept of distance and the possibility of being in contact even if one was apart. The object remained. His characters could now set off on adventures with a "check-back" to mummy, who remained in reality, although at sufficient distance so that he was able to try his own wings.

Many children whom we meet have not, for various reasons, been able to work with nearness–distance. There has sometimes been an intense experience of closeness between mother and child. The early experience of distance has not been able to occur with the mother present. Instead, this has occurred in connection with a real and abrupt separation.

Reflecting space

Viktor's mother had great difficulty in thinking about his *inner world*. What she saw frightened her, and her own fantasy, which she needed in order to try to explore what was going on inside him, was not accessible to her. Perhaps she had never been allowed to develop this side of herself. When we offered his mother a "talking-therapy" (with the parental psychotherapist) this was therefore not a good way of reaching this family. Talking therapy assumes that there is an experience of a *space* in which an *I* and a *you* can meet and reflect over certain phenomena (an embryo of a triangle). If one is unable to perceive that a physical space also includes an experience of distance, "in the mind", then the conversation will not become a billowing dance between two parties but a debate like a response to another person's comments. One is unable to comprehend that the other person thinks, feels, reflects within himself, and that what comes out as a question does not necessarily imply the truth. The parental psychotherapist worked a great deal with this reflecting space in the sessions, both by being a model and also by concretely exploring this new field together with Viktor's mother. In my room Viktor began to endure, and gradually became fascinated by, concepts such as "We'll see", and "I wonder if . . .".

Through my holding comments he was able to endure the fact that solutions were not immediately at hand. It became possible for him to complete the sessions with "to be continued next Thursday", which it also was.

In the beginning his games had been repetitive, in a compulsive way; later on he tried to discover new dimensions. He ascertained that a boat, which had floated on the water in the sand-tray, was the same boat that had sunk and lay on the bottom. He had read about *Wasa*. (*Wasa* was the pride of the Swedish fleet and was lost on her maiden voyage, in 1628.) At first he said that he was there when the ship sank—not in fantasy, but as he conveyed it, he was there! Later on he was able to fantasize about *Wasa* more and more. He established that one could see his pretend *Wasa* at the bottom in the sand-tray, despite the fact that it was *below* the surface of the water.

During one period he often drew pictures. From not having been able to draw at all, came pictures in which he liked to show, with very clear lines indicating speed, how cannon balls *from* a pirate ship flew over the water *to* another vessel. Movement and power that showed distance could now be both perceived in his mind and represented in drawings and in play, and he began to show an interest in sharing these experiences with me.

It is when a child is first able to comprehend concepts such as *behind that*; *here*; *in front of that*; that a concept of time can be established. The experience of the meaning of the concepts of *prepositions* thus needs to exist both in the body and in the mind before a notion of time is possible. How can one comprehend *then*, *now*, *later*, if one is unable to understand the meaning of psychological distance? In Alvarez and Reid's book *Autism and Personality* (1999), Youell describes the difference between "knowledge" (to mechanically express knowledge, repetition of facts) and "knowing" (an ability that involves a mind that can think). It is when there is "knowing" that knowledge is not just repetitive, but bears meaning and is generalizable, an emotional knowledge.

How one develops emotional cognition—a clinical example

Amando came to me when he was three years old. He was carried in naked, clinging convulsively to his mother's necklace, which he pressed in his hand. He was laid down on the floor, staring quietly into the lamp and fiddling with the necklace. Every attempt by his father to intervene led to any possible activity freezing to ice. In his mother's embrace he became one with her. The only way to comfort him (and that was often necessary) was to carry him around. He was large for his age, and my first intervention was to help the parents find a place where they could sit a little comfortably and not walk around carrying this child who was far too heavy on the back and arms. It was thus important to find a "facilitating environment" for the parents from which they could reach out to their child and begin to offer him a stable container and a secure base from which to start out.

For a long time it was impossible to separate the parents and child. Amando "went to pieces" in front of my eyes when he was without his mother or a piece of her jewellery. I therefore worked only with one parent at a time together with the boy in my room. My interventions were much of a "reverie". I thought aloud about what I saw. This was my only possible position. I was unable to reach out to the boy. But it was also a conscious strategy through which to create a reflecting space with the parents, in which there was sufficient distance for thoughts to be able to exist, be shared and further developed.

To fall to pieces and to be able to play at falling to pieces

Amando showed time after time that he did not have any tools with which to manage a physical or psychological distance. He was also unable to remain in a situation of nearness when a parent tried to initiate the embryo of an attempt at contact. At first I turned exclusively to the parents and worked via them. "I wonder if Amando doesn't . . .?" "Did you see that when you did that, it seemed as if Amando actually heard what you said . . .?" I tried to bring meaning to what was being played out in front of my eyes. Amando went to pieces when the towers that his mother tried to build fell as soon as he touched them. The same thing happened when a bit of a puzzle did not fit. All activity ceased, his body fell into total collapse on the floor and he screamed with anxiety. He was not angry or frightened of something. He did not yet have the capacity to think of something else. He was therefore unable to be scared of anything, an enemy, out there. Everything in and around him seemed to be huge, catastrophic dangers. The experience of an unspeakable horror, "nameless dread" (Bion, 1962b), was constantly present. This was so all-embracing that it did not have a representation. It could not be seen at a distance. It just was. It was in the boy, in the room, in the parents, and in me. It was completely impossible to find words for what I saw.

After a little more than a term of parent–child therapy on a once weekly basis Amando had so much experience of himself that he was able to be alone with me. He then came three times a week, one of these sessions together with one of his parents. For a long time we worked with the aim of helping him perceive and accept his father, and not only mummy, as a potential helper.

He began to understand distance (not being the same) in a very concrete way. In the beginning he lumbered up and down the stairs, his energy could be exhausted at any time and he could sink to the floor. I had to actively drag him to his feet again. After a time of monotonous lumbering, I wearied of our perpetual performance and without thinking about it began to rhythmically jump a little between the steps, mostly to keep myself mentally alert. I noticed to my surprise how Amando responded by jumping in the same way, but in a slower tempo. This developed into an interplay between us. For a while the stairs became the most important intermediate area. He and I sounded like elephants when we thumped down! In this joint rhythm it became possible to introduce different rhythms, I could jump quicker or take two steps on the same stair. Through this Amando began to "socialize" with things in the world. He almost never smiled and it was difficult to get a glimpse of his look. However, we met in the joint rhythm that he could tolerate and he could be pleased that the rhythm was sometimes not identical between us. A physical, and an embryo to mental, distance was established.

I had a need to introduce something *between us* in the form of a bit of paper and a crayon. I used to make simple sketches of what he was doing in the room or where I was seated. At first he drew nothing. I felt ridiculous sitting there trying to show that this was possible. However, slowly Amando imitated my attempts to hold the crayon and began to draw a few lines. After a while they became figures who looked like one-eyed tennis rackets. Amando wanted to tape them all up on the wall, one beside the other (it was again me that had shown that this was possible). He soon taped them *over* one another, *three dimensionally*, like the pages of a calendar. Quite soon he had the idea that he wanted to cut out the characters with the scissors. Cognitively, and with subtle motor activity, he practised cutting out, but on an emotional plane he had discovered that one actually could *cut* something (a figure) *out of* something else. The foreground (the essential part) was cut out so that the background remained (the rest of the paper). *An emotional cognition* was possible and a mental representation of the concept of separation was established. Parallel with this it became possible for Amando to play that something got broken in order to repair and restore it. The world did not break if he took something apart. Amando was now able to perceive that *he* was an agent. He was the one that carried out an action and in that way *actively* interplayed with the surrounding world.

Later—what is that?

With Amando I could also follow the formation of emotional concepts with regard to the comprehension of time. The word "later" was imbued with a meaning in the form of "Yes, we shall meet again", or "Not now, but you can do it later". These simple sentences became like a mantra for the concept "It'll be all right". I do not believe that it carried a meaning of time, but was just an assurance of predictability.

On one occasion Amando went in front of me down the winding staircase. Suddenly he said: "Britta later". I assured him that I was behind him, but he looked intensely at me (this was one of the first time our eyes met) and he repeated, "No, Britta *later*". It took me some time before I realized that he wanted to go ahead of me, round the bend in the stairs, so that we couldn't see each other. I let him pass behind the bend, out of sight, and I heard him exclaim, "Britta, now!" He had never used that word before. He looked very satisfied. He had now started to be an agent in his own right, who had achieved some capacity to regulate the distance to someone else.

On an other occasion Amando was very sad and cried in an adequate manner for his mummy, who was in her session in the parental psychotherapist's room adjacent to mine. He now had a capacity to comprehend distance and therewith the feeling that the object was not present. He had come so far in his development of a unified "self" that I chose to stay with him in my room. He rushed towards the door and cried for his mummy. I emphasized that mummy was in the other room talking and that we would go to her *later.* He cried, but sank down into a sitting position by the door. He let me sink down beside him, and we shared the grief over his mummy not being accessible just now. I told him what I thought his mummy and the therapist were doing. In this way I wanted to show him that it is possible to retain the object in the mind and to think about it, even if one is not physically present with each other. It was sad for Amando, but not devastating. He "himself" remained and this "self" was able to lament something else (something *outside* him). We shared an emotional meaning (missing, longing) of what was probably felt in Amando and looked together at the Kleenex becoming wet with his tears. I think this was one of the first times he could actually see that something (the wet tears) came *from him* and that they had something to do with his mother not being right beside him. He could exist without her, although this was a sad experience.

Out there

For a long time Amando did not have the ability to comprehend that an "out there" existed. He was unable to spit, unable to speak, unable to blow his nose, unable to throw anything away. He could not keep food in his mouth and chew it. It just slipped down his throat, straight into his stomach. He could put a boiled tortellini in his mouth and a second later it was in his stomach without even being chewed. The whole of him comprised a direction *into* him. When he tried (quite awkwardly) to play with bat and ball, he moved slowly with the bat in his hand after the ball as if annihilating all notion of distance between the ball and the bat. He was unable to shoot away the ball. He simply did not know how one carried out such a manoeuvre. He snuffled inward, cleared his throat roughly, struck himself with his hands inwards towards his stomach. He tried to blow soap bubbles, which was not physically possible for him. When his mother blew for him, he spent all his energy in bursting the bubbles as soon as they left her mouth. I had to actively hold him while the mother blew, and with words help him to begin to discover the phenomenon that one can look *at* something, observe something *at* a distance. Mummy remained, despite the fact that the bubble left her mouth. After a time of working with this concept, it became possible for him to (physically) blow away bubbles himself. He could stand for a long time and watch them as they floated away in the room and out on the balcony.

Through the discovery that he (actively himself) was able to take himself down the stairs jumping, he discovered a movement *out from, away from*. I believe that this had been unexplored for him as his earlier history was related to real loss of close objects. When he was able to understand the direction *outwards*, it became possible, for the first time, for him to project and represent inner experiences and he began to draw coherent sequences of pictures, like a cartoon. Amando now had a mind of his own.

Theory of mind and the subjunctive

The grammatical form of the subjunctive (conjunctive) illustrates what *a theory* may mean. Theories are not facts, but hypotheses about certain phenomena that one tries to bring together under more generalizing or abstract concepts. In order to achieve this, it is assumed that one, in the mind, is able to comprehend the linguistic verb form of the subjunctive (Latin, *coniunctivus irrealis*). In the word "irrealis" it emerges that the hypothesis, the theories, the thoughts, are not for real, but an attempt to find a way into a world that does not contain truths. If we shall be able to comprehend and comment that something *seems* (appears) to exist on the inside of another person (that he or she has thoughts, feelings) we must first be able to perceive that *inside* is something that has a meaning for us. Here we have that which I have just described about how a mind develops. The next part is being able to understand that inside a person is not the same thing as inside me. It is also not the same thing as outside. In many languages the subjunctive form of the verb has a special inflection (often imperfect) that indicates to the receiver of the message the understanding that the sentence is not a "truth" but something that *could perhaps be* a point of departure for continued conversation. "For Christmas I wished I had . . ." has another meaning than "For Christmas I am going to have . . .".

Parental psychotherapy and the subjunctive

Another question concerning the concept of the theory of mind emerges in our work with the children's parents. Many parents can fantasize and think about their child, others have great difficulties in doing so. In the sessions with the parents we suggest that they should *reflect* together with the parental psychotherapist. We presuppose that those parents we have in front of us are able and willing to reflect, think about a phenomenon, an event, a problem: their child. To think about is not the same thing as to think (Bion, 1962b). All parents are able to think, and the care around a child may be very good. But what does it mean to think *about* someone? This presupposes that one believes that the other has an inner life (Waddell, 1998), and one does not know with certainty how this inner life represents itself. In order to be able to understand the inside of one's new-born child, parents start out from their "reverie" about their child. Through projections and empathic ability, they try to register and interpret what can be thought to be going on *inside* the child. One does not know with certainty. "He is hungry" is perhaps a right thought about the child's condition, but it may also be that he is screaming for some other reason.

When we suggest "talking" as a form of psychotherapy, we assume the existence of a reflecting mind, with a wish for a space between two persons in which it is possible to talk over the child's difficulties and parenthood to this particular child. But we also suggest that we should talk "irrealis", that is to say that we shall *think about* something we do not know to be true. However, we want, together with the parents, to explore what may perhaps convey meaning in the child's odd behaviour.

It is therefore of the greatest importance that we think about the language with which parents are able or want to talk to us. Some wish to embark upon a voyage of discovery, even if it entails encountering old horrors. Others are unable or do not wish to talk in this way. In these particular cases working with parent and child together may be an accessible method. They can then, together, in front of each other's eyes and in their bodies, experience phenomena such as nearness, distance, being able to think about something, share this, and also, one hopes, meet and deal with this "something".

Time and space: position, subject, predicate, object, prepositions, adjectives, and adverbs

Through the emotional experience of distance, the two children I have described were able for the first time to find a *position* from where they could observe the world, a point of departure, a "secure base". It is only when this capacity is established that the child is able to begin *to observe* the world as something *out there.* To observe, register, contemplate, "think about", the surrounding world is possible when we have a fixed starting point. The surrounding world can become precisely that, a *surrounding* world, and not a part of one's self. Systematizing and time sequences can be discovered and explored.

The experience of one's own position in the world is the point of departure for subsequently being able to see how other people move *in relation* to one another and towards oneself. It becomes possible to discover the concept of *preposition.* It is first when a child is able to comprehend that someone (a subject) does something (a predicate) to someone else (an object) that it becomes possible on a deeper level to understand the meaning of adjectives and adverbs. Characters may be different, they can do things in various ways and it is possible to compare them.

Children like Viktor and Amando are totally occupied with discovering that they are subjects. All the other phenomena concerning distance and relationship are still too difficult to conceptualize.

When the experience of being a subject exists, then this subject is able to *do* something (a predicate). This means that the child is an *agent*, someone who is able to perform an activity. The first step in the formation of the concept that one can *do* something comprises a perception of the *present* form of the verb. For both Victor and Amando, as well as other children with similar difficulties that I have met during the years, the next stage in the perception of time is that something can take place further on, later. There is a *future* in the form of an assurance that there exists a life outside and ahead of the present. It is when they are first able to comprehend that one can *share* one's experiences with other objects that it becomes possible for them to relate their everyday experiences in the *imperfect* tense. They have developed a self-perception, a mind, which makes it possible to remember and retell for another being something they have experienced (Stern, 1985). It was then that I was first able to help these two children to understand that there are objects, other people, or characters in the surrounding world.

A long time later, when it became possible for them to understand that these people or figures could have various characteristics, adjectives and adverbs became possible concepts to explore. It became possible to compare various phenomena. Only then could a theory of mind be established.

Acknowledgements

I should like to express my gratitude to psychotherapist Ulla Hörsta, Sweden, who helped me many years ago to get a hint of the work with children with autism. Also my warmest thanks to Dr Giuliana De Astis, Italy, who supervised me in such a generous and rewarding way. Finally, my thanks goes to psychotherapist Anne Alvarez, UK, who has inspired so many of us to try to understand more about the minds of children like the ones described in this article.

CHAPTER THREE

The symbolic and the concrete: psychotic adolescents in psychoanalytic psychotherapy[1]

Julia Pestalozzi

Unique disturbances in symbolization are characteristic of the pathology of schizophrenia. Drawing on the case vignette of a psychotic adolescent, I discuss theoretical problems in the symbolization process in general and then in psychosis, in particular the relation between "concretism" as a thought disorder and other psychotic defences. The ability to symbolize, on the one hand, and to maintain sufficiently stable ego boundaries on the other, are examined in their relation. My clinical experience supports my hypothesis that there is a close relationship between the impairment of the symbolization process in the adolescent or adult psychotic patient and his/her inability to engage in symbolic play as a child. Special attention is paid to the role of early trauma and consequent pathology of object relations for disturbances of symbolic play in childhood. Regression to concrete thinking is understood as the chance of the psychotic patient to give some meaning to reality in an unreal, delusional world and as his/her last chance to communicate at all. Conclusions are drawn for psychoanalytic techniques in the treatment of patients who are deeply regressed in this respect. Special attention is given to the particular circumstances and challenges of adolescence and to providing psychoanalytic psychotherapy to adolescent psychotic patients.

To illustrate my argument I should like to start by considering the story of a nineteen-year-old psychotic adolescent at the start of his treatment in psychoanalytic psychotherapy.[2] At the time I started writing this chapter, the patient had been in treatment for about six months, twice per week, face to face. When I refer to him as a "psychotic adolescent" I mean that he was a "psychotically functioning adolescent" as termed by Laufer and Laufer (1984)—i.e., a youth whose condition includes psychiatrically-defined psychotic symptoms (not just a "psychotic core" in a psychoanalytic sense), but whose psychotic symptoms can be described with some therapeutic optimism as being in such flow and as so closely knit with the issues of adolescence and as a dramatic response to such that they may be appropriately regarded rather as a form of "psychotic functioning" than a case of fully established schizophrenia. The same symptoms occurring in a patient twenty years older would undoubtedly be classified as schizophrenia.

Referring to this case history and to other vignettes, I will proceed to:

(a) discuss theoretical problems in the symbolization process in general and then, in particular, in psychosis;
(b) outline some models that are of help to me in visualizing psychotic events and ordering them from the perspective of developmental psychology;
(c) examine styles of therapeutic intervention in the light of the above considerations; and
(d) illustrate why I believe the period of adolescence, especially in the heat of a florid psychosis and specifically via psychotic transference in the therapeutic setting, represents a huge, perhaps unrepeatable, opportunity for psychoanalytic psychotherapy to be effective.

Daniel

Daniel was referred to me by a colleague because he complained of having "lost" his feelings as of about two years ago. Once an unusually gifted student and literary talent, he had come to maintain just a shadowy existence in school.

In my reception room there sits a very well-behaved, well-groomed "intellectual" youth. Before entering the office for the first time, he asks me if he can bring his backpack along with him, and I find myself automatically fetching my own backpack from the hallway corridor as well. Later in this chapter I shall further address this initial (obviously countertransferential) action of mine. Daniel's gait, stiff posture, and "locked-up" facial expression give his appearance almost a catatonic quality. He sits before me as if in prison, his hands laid carefully on his thighs, half in expectation, half in defence. "You asked if you could bring your backpack with you into the office", I note. And then I continue, "Maybe you have a wish to try to get things in your backpack a bit into order?", thereby expressing myself in the symbolic style of a normal neurotic analyst. ("Backpack" is frequently used metaphorically in German to mean that which burdens us in life.) He points to the backpack and answers, seemingly without registering the symbolic ambiguity of my question but giving clear expression to his psychotic ego disturbance, "Yes. It's falling apart. There are holes everywhere, and you can stick your hands through all the pockets." What is happening here? The patient is speaking concretely, I metaphorically; yet we nevertheless seem to understand one another. This paper will focus on this special form of symbolic–non-symbolic communication[3] between psychotic patient and analyst.

Daniel goes on to tell me that he is distanced from everything and he feels a "total lack of emotional involvement". He always knows how he is *supposed* to be feeling, and when other people seem happy or sad he tries, but he himself feels nothing. His thoughts also do not flow naturally—sometimes they seem to be stalled, and then the images just run away from him. He is unable to concentrate on anything, to penetrate a problem, to think about anything in depth—he must perpetually watch the way his own mind works. And, also, his head is "covered in armour". After listening to his description for a while, I finally ask him if, perhaps, his feelings are so difficult and so threatening that they have to be kept safe behind that armour. At that he seems to become a bit livelier and he remarks, "Yes, mainly fear."

This short passage is packed full of material that elicits a number of questions. What does Daniel mean when he says his "head is covered in armour"? For me, as a non-psychotic person, and for most other people, this is a metaphor for a state of being trapped. As we know, many beautiful, vivid metaphors make reference to our elementary physical experience and thereby generate a certain playful intimacy between speaker and listener. Metaphors are a communication medium *par excellence*.[4] In line with psychoanalytical thinking, I extend the inherent ambiguity of the metaphor of the armour (ambiguity is part of the normal usage of symbols and metaphors) to its war related associations: I sense destructive potential. My experience with schizophrenic patients also tells me that this picture speaks of Daniel's ego boundaries, as represented in the body schema, as very frail and therefore in need of being reinforced and over cathected by the coat of armour. Thus, the word "armour" possesses a rich and vivid symbolic aura for me, allowing a chain of different meanings to be generated according to the communicative situation. And precisely this is the nature of metaphors.

But what does Daniel mean when he speaks of "armour"? He is not a psychosomatic patient, for whom it would mean nothing. Nor is he a neurotic headache patient, who would use the word "armour" descriptively in an "as if" sense. He is also not a classic schizophrenic patient who would believe in a *real* suit of armour made of iron or steel, in the sense of Segal's "symbolic equation".[5] No, Daniel is a typical adolescent psychotic with the "ability to doubt" as described by Laufer and Laufer (1984, p. 194). And, yet, what we perceive as a metaphor is something *concrete* for Daniel and this "concretism" or the "concrete attitude" (Josephs, 1989) is typical of a schizophrenic communication situation. Daniel experiences this part of his body, this "skull of armour", as something very concrete, a part of him split from the rest, a loose fragment that has a life of its own. Daniel later reports that at one spot this skull also has a hole into which anybody can reach. For us, this image is an impressive depiction of the gaps in the solid, protecting ego boundaries, where projective identifications can freely pass back and forth, a symbol of psychotic breakdown (it is not uncommon for psychotics to refer to holes—holes in the body, in the landscape, even in the air). The hole may also express the fear of intrusion by the psychotherapist, which Daniel already intimated in his reference to the backpack. However, Daniel perceives this as an actual hole in the concrete sense.

This also applies to the *feelings* Daniel describes as being extinguished, "lost". It is not, as would be in the case of a schizoid person, that Daniel has feelings about which he knows nothing. Rather, he describes his emotions as having been segregated from the rest of his psychic existence, and where they once resided he now feels a gap. He is missing a piece of himself. This gives Daniel the feeling that he is insane. And, in fact, he is. Because even these lost feelings he perceives in concrete terms. This concrete feature of his thinking—and this is the point I want to emphasize in this introduction—is what makes his thinking psychotic. Later in the paper I will attempt to demonstrate that a fascinating and challenging aspect of conducting therapy with psychotic patients is "learning to understand this concrete thinking in both concrete *and* metaphorical terms while initially responding in concrete terms in closest contact with the patient's own imagery within the secure boundaries of the patient's symptoms" (Benedetti, 1983, p. 73). For example, I responded to Daniel's report of the hole in his skull, which I, of course, also understood in its transferential context, as follows: "Then we both have to make sure that I don't reach in too far with my words, and you have to help me to keep this from happening."

Another essential symptom of Daniel's is an "inner voice". It is not a hallucination in the strict sense, but it is far more concrete than that which *we* mean when we refer to an "inner voice", i.e., the voice of our conscience. Daniel's inner voice, as I only later came to realize, was more of a dull, awful sensation that only "became speech" in the course of psychotherapy. This voice comments negatively on everything that Daniel does: "You can't do it right, anyway, you're too stupid, just give up". This voice is so powerful that it prevents him from getting out of bed in the morning or opening his mouth in the company of peers—thus, he usually remains silent. Daniel is under virtually permanent surveillance by the voice and is harassed and tortured by it. Sleep is his only refuge. But he awakens in the morning with a feeling of complete helplessness and he dreads the coming day ("I am trampled, crushed . . ."). He reports: "I am hardly able to get up in the morning. I feel small and helpless. My skin is too thin . . . Afraid of total failure . . . then the voice comes, and the eyes from above." Not surprisingly, his time spent at school is completely unproductive. He is tolerated there despite his near catatonic state only because of the brilliance of his earlier academic performance.

This inner voice devalues Daniel, and, as we later come to see, it does so with an attitude of the sublime. It seemingly sets itself above all else, which is treated as absolutely meaningless, and it comments on the sheer futility of every undertaking. In this voice we can recognize a personification of Rosenfeld's destructive narcissism (1987) or the arrogant, destructive, dependency-creating aspect of the so-called "psychic retreat" described by Steiner (1993). But, at the same time, in the presence of this voice Daniel is never alone, and being left alone is excruciating for him. This is another of Daniel's symptoms. He suffers terribly when his parents are out of the house; he is dependent on their real, physical presence, as he will very quickly also come to need my real presence. Bringing sessions to a conclusion becomes an ongoing technical problem in the therapy. As he clings to the words I speak, and struggles to keep my eye contact with him from ever wavering, he clings to the door handle, speaking just one more sentence, asking just one more question: "Do you think things will improve? Couldn't the reason for this be that . . .?" Absence can be made bearable through symbolization, by forming a representation of the "other" that keeps the person present to us in the realm of thought. But for this patient, absence is experienced as a void, and this void is a sort of inner death; a state in which all meaning has ceased.

I gradually become familiar with three aspects of Daniel's inner world: a figure that we both refer to as the "opponent", the "inner sadist", the "mafioso", or the "killer". This figure "thinks" for Daniel, but in a perverted, destructive manner that acts to paralyse real, deeper-going thought. It either comments on Daniel's actual thinking, will, or action in a stereotypically negative manner, or it "breaks everything apart". It describes this, for example, as follows: "Others might go out on the street and smash up whatever they find. But I destroy things in another way, I dismember them—when I'm talking with people I see just the mouth or the jaw moving up and down, or the eyes, or their spoken words appear in capital letters in front of my eyes . . . oh, that's so terrible . . .". In this way, the other person as a whole remains out of reach, leaving Daniel hopelessly alone with his sadistic protector. He describes it like this: "Either I'm inside and then I'm completely cut off [schizophrenic autism], or I'm open and then everything just rushes into me with such a force that I can't keep it under control at all, and my head is just full of stuff . . . *I'm like an animal in a wire cage.*" The image of the cage indicates that the "inner opponent" also offers Daniel some form of protection, as a second skin might hold together Daniel's fragile, cracked ego boundaries—but it is made of barbed wire, with the barbs facing outward and inward.

Behind this figure is the second dimension, a gaping, deadly void. The patient's sensation that he can no longer think or feel anything or explore a problem, his delusional perception of being five centimetres outside his own body, his fear and his freezing when his parents are not home or our session comes to an end—these are all allusions to an inner death. Gradually, we discover Daniel's uncanny ability to virtually read other people's thoughts and finish their sentences for them, including my own. He soon learns to practically take the words right out of my mouth. Initially, I am delighted at what seems to be so much intuitive understanding of my good ideas, but then a twofold defensive aspect becomes apparent. First of all, by linking into communication with me this way, as long as we speak he is protected from feelings of loneliness, abandonment, and emptiness (after a few weeks in therapy, he is stricken by fear if I even divert my glance from him, and he hardly tolerates brief pauses in the conversation). But from the long threads that we spin together in our talks, he weaves a cocoon, i.e., the insights that we gain together in the therapy at first do not really sink in and, therefore, they cannot help or "warm" him after the session. It is as if an inner space that could connect with an outer object emotionally and cognitively has been rendered dead. Thus, not only the true inner dependency on the outer object is denied but also Daniel's own living self. This makes it very difficult to "learn from experience". Daniel's demonic companion, the "inner voice" (Rosenfeld's "gang", 1971), is effective in protecting him from my entering that "dead" inner space.

Second, there is a small, suffering Daniel who shows up from time to time, a tortured, terrorized little victim—Daniel who is afraid he might not make it, who hides himself anxiously in a shell, who, when I divert my eyes from him during therapy or during my holiday breaks, not only *is* alone but also *feels* alone. Here lies the source of hope for this patient, I believe. Here, I can address the victim side of Daniel and together we can talk about his mafioso side. Of course, at present, this aggressor side is an enforcement of Daniel's identity and essential to his survival. Bearing this in mind, I try very carefully to denounce this destructive, killing side, while at the same time taking advantage of the closeness that becomes established between Daniel and me (which, of course, will also have to be analysed one day). I aim to give inner reinforcement to his feeling, suffering side, which is still capable of relating, by attempting to instil his pain with an aspect of dignity. I, for instance, frequently pointed out how empty, stereotyped and thoughtless his quasi-automated self-denigrations were, as compared to the warm, lively, humane, and sometimes poetic quality of his suffering. I shared with him implicitly my conviction that endurance and respect for mental pain and sorrow has a quality that lies at the root of artistic creativity as much as of human solidarity. This technique—heavily leaning on Benedetti's technical modifications—obviously involves communications on the part of the therapist, which, dealing with non-psychotic patients, could rightly be taxed with being "narcissistic gratifications"; with their obvious bias such communications are not *sensu strictu* "neutral" either (see Benedetti, 1983, p. 77).The grief of separation in the transference (not the panic of nameless separation anxiety) will lead our way back to the hidden world of lost feelings.[6]

Now I would now like to turn to Daniel's history.

Anamnesis

Daniel was the long awaited first child of warm-hearted, caring parents. At the age of one month, he had to be hospitalized due to an exfoliative dermatitis (a staphylococcal infection) that covered more than a third of his body. The condition was critical and his chances of survival were uncertain. For three months he was kept isolated in a glass incubator; his mother was not allowed to touch him. Lumbar punctures were carried out daily. Afterwards, the relationship between mother and child was, as the mother herself described, "too close". She could not divert her attention from her once nearly lost child and he, on his part, sought her presence whenever possible. They intuited one another's feelings, understood one another "without words"—a form of communication very different from that with the father: verbal, matter-of-fact, and manly. Even during latency, Daniel wanted her presence most of the time, and he developed bizarre and quasi delusional fears of being abandoned by his parents. There is no scope in this paper to refer to the oedipal implications of all this, which became relevant at much later phases of the therapy.

Daniel had always been a "special child". He was ambitious and insisted on playing only with real tools and other items; he completely rejected ordinary toys and role-playing games. "He was totally uncompromising," says his mother. He was a lonely child, and the only friendship he had during primary school ended suddenly and painfully following a narcissistic injury. At high school he had a few crushes on girls. He was an expert learner in all subjects and an outstanding cello player, but he always remained on the periphery of his peer group. A year before starting therapy he had begun suffering from impairments of concentration, his performance at school plummeted, and his entire existence seemed to become paralysed.

Two aspects of this history are of particular note for our considerations here: first of all, of course, the very early and extended life-threatening trauma that Daniel suffered; and then his inability to engage in symbolic games later in childhood.

The concrete

Let us start with the second point. I am fascinated by the fact that I not infrequently encounter this detail in the histories of psychotic patients, yet I do not find any reference to it in the literature.[7] Clinically, most adolescent and adult schizophrenics appear to have been more or less "normal" children. They acquire normal language and the use of thousands of different metaphors. None the less, as children they are unable to engage in symbolic play. Not until adolescence, when psychosis manifests, usually as schizophrenia, is the eminent human ability to create meaning through metaphor lost.[8] I suggest that there is a close relationship between the impairment of the symbolization process in the adolescent or adult psychotic patient and the inability to engage in symbolic play as a child. This would appear to be important, as it might illuminate essential aspects of the psychodynamics and psychogenesis of psychosis.

Before exploring this relationship, I would like to examine in detail the disturbances in the symbolization process exhibited by the adult psychotic, which were briefly addressed in the introduction.

We have noted that in psychosis, particularly schizophrenia, the ability to flexibly differentiate between the concrete and the symbolic is impaired: on the one hand, the psychotic mind tends to understand the symbolic–metaphorical in concrete terms, in the sense of Segal's "symbolic equation". On the other hand, concrete entities get over-charged with animistic–metaphorical meaning that is not consistent with their communicative valence. Simple objects become fantastically meaningful. There is an inflation of what at first glance would appear to be the symbolic but, indeed, it is not. In these cases, the patient is no longer able to distinguish between the signified and the signifier, i.e., between the image and its meaning (see Benedetti, 1992, pp. 33–34).

Drawing on interaction theory, modern linguistics teaches us that a normal, healthy person is able to distinguish between the concrete and the metaphorical according to the communicative situation in question.[9] This occurs naturally and fluently. We can, for instance, understand a rose in the hand of a person simply as a rose, a flower. Or, on the basis of projective testing of the feelings of that person, we can interpret the rose as an expression of love. This playful switch is what the psychotic person loses for the simple-sounding reason that he/she is no longer able to empathize successfully with either real or imagined others (see Caper, 1999, pp. 86–90). In order to determine whether a rose someone is holding, for example, is simply a rose and nothing more, or is rather an outright sign of love, or perhaps a symbolic expression of unconscious love, I have to be able to rely on my so-called "normal" or "realistic" or "communicative" projective identification. To empathize I must be able to make my way into the inner world of the other, to feel what the other person feels. And the fantasies I create of the situation must be calibrated by other signs of that person's objective reality. This is not always so easy. I must not project too much, otherwise my ego boundaries are compromised with the resulting confusion as described by Rosenfeld (1971). But I must not project too little either, otherwise I shall not understand anything, there is nothing to find out, nothing to interpret, nothing to play with; then I will be alexithymic in the truest sense of the word. To be sane, I must be able to "test" my projections on the object and to probe and make experimental identifications, never forgetting that the "other" is, indeed, another person different and separate from me.[10] And if the projection does not seem to fit with his/her reality, then I need to be able to withdraw it and know that—alas!—it was just my fantasy. This is how we orientate ourselves in talking to others and in our imagination all the time; this is how we function as analysts; this is also how we love our sexual partners, who are so different and yet so similar to ourselves; this is also how we deal with inanimate objects, by setting our fears and wishes in relation to their reality, testing them, pushing them to their limits. In the tradition of Bion this is regarded as "normal, communicative projective identification".

This projective identification can live with ambiguity and uncertainties, it can be withdrawn, and it can tolerate absence and create a symbolic substitute for the absent object. This playful, yet securely anchored orientation, is often lost in psychosis when—contrary to common assumption—fantasy and the ability to symbolize and interpret fail. Why? In the Kleinian tradition, to which I adhere in most ways, one would say that the power of the inner objects is so great and dreadful that they have to be evacuated with omnipotent force. When inner objects (part objects) are too powerful, projections and projective identification become too strong. It is the forceful, evacuating projection of intolerable contents that causes splitting, leads to the dissolution of ego boundaries, and to a confusion of self and other, of past and present, and of the real object and its symbolic representation (Rosenfeld, 1952, p. 117; see also Rodrigué, 1956, p. 147). The use of symbols—which always entails an act of substitution of something absent—is lost.[11] To symbolize, the self must have a degree of invariance (Benedetti, personal communication) and the object, as noted by Bion, must be able to be perceived as a whole (Bion, 1953, p. 26). In other words, the ability to symbolize, on the one hand, and to maintain sufficiently stable ego boundaries while perceiving whole objects, on the other, may be regarded as different sides of the same coin. If all this is lost, non-symbolic concrete thinking will take over to fill the gap.

The following episode provides an example of how concrete thinking functions when true interpersonal orientation is lacking, i.e, when there is an inability to empathize properly. For a number of years I have been treating an adult patient, chronically schizophrenic, though socially well integrated, who is a trained nurse. Recently she suddenly said, "You know, I understand you well . . . when you touch your ear it means you hear me, when you scratch your nose it means you are 'wrinkling your nose at me', when you touch your eyes you are saying that you really see me, and when you touch your mouth you are saying, 'That's good—it has to do with orality'." What is happening here? Is this thinking symbolic or non-symbolic? I would argue that this is pseudo-symbolism, used as a clumsy crutch in a moment of affective–cognitive disorientation, because in this session, for various reasons, the normal orientation, the empathy, the use of projecting probing failed once again and the patient was unable to reconstruct a coherent representation of me from the many symbolic inputs she received over the years. To compensate for her lack of orientation, the patient latches on to isolated movements of mine, which to me are completely meaningless and she imbues them with ponderous meaning unnegotiable at the moment. Here, we are not witnessing a true symbolization process, but the construction of brittle, disjoined signs. We may better understand this patient's desperate tendency to create meaning this way if we know that prior to therapy she suffered a long-lasting, acute delusional state. In her confusion, the world was constantly experienced as unreal. In this unreal, delusional world, concrete thinking can help create a feeling that reality is tangible, comprehensible, unequivocal.

Symbolic play

The child's ordinary symbolic play is, I believe, the rich context in which we learn and practise distinguishing between projection and external reality (Caper, 1999, pp. 86–88).

The scope of this paper permits only a brief outline of the origins and development of symbolization in childhood. Freud saw symbolization from the perspective of positive "wish fulfilment" (gratification of a drive, which is able to circumvent censure by means of displacement, condensation, etc.). Klein understood it as an "escape" from sadistically charged internal object relations. But both Freud and Klein placed the developmental origins of the processes of identification and projection, and thus the origin of substitutive symbolic representation, in the period of earliest infancy. Today we know, on the basis of Piaget's studies (Piaget & Inhelder, 1969), the work of the interpersonalists like Sullivan (1953), and the observations made by Stern, Brazelton, and their school (Stern, 1985), that this dating is not tenable. In fact, the strength of the infant lies in its very concrete-orientated perception of reality. It begins life as an "excellent reality tester" (Stern, 1985, p. 11), and its perceptions are neither distorted by projections nor by symbols, but at most by the immaturity of its cognitive capacities. Otherwise the infant would not be able to learn as quickly as it does. Imagination and thus symbolization do not manifest until the second year of life, at about the same time as the semiotic function. Piaget's earlier "sensorimotor" phase is thus pre-imaginative and proto-symbolic,[12] i.e., concrete. The engrammes established during this phase do not, according to Lorenzer, consist of individual objects, but are "scenic" in character, determined by the needs of the child and by the rules of interaction in the maternal environment. For this reason, one speaks of "determined" forms of interaction. They are represented in concrete, scenic, sensorimotor forms of interaction (e.g., in the tender interactive stimulation associated with feeding, in frustration situations).[13] This "determined interaction" (Lorenzer, 1970) refers to the deepest level of the schematization of reality (according to pleasure and pain values) in the subject. The basal structuring of the personality through acquisition of determined forms of interaction influences the symbolization process in so far as these forms of interaction are maintained as a fundamental layer of meaning even after the symbolization function is fully developed. In other words, "deferred", they come to form a layer of "meaning" once they are incorporated as a physical need into the symbolic forms (Schmid Noerr, 2000, pp. 466–470). Not until then, i.e., until the second year of life, do the "determined forms of interaction" become "symbolic forms of interaction" that permit the child to deal with reality independently of its real presence. This phase is therefore decisive for certain affective and cognitive structures that form the basis of "representational thinking".[14] Stern's findings (1985) are much in line with this.

In many respects, the so-called "concrete attitude" encountered among psychosomatic and psychotic patients is quite similar in functioning to the "concretism" of the sensorimotor phase.

I would contend, in agreement with authors like Searles (1968, pp. 575–583), Josephs (1989, pp. 484–90) and Jackson (Jackson & Williams, 1994), that persons who eventually become psychotic, such as the nurse described above, or Daniel, who sees only the chattering jaw or the eyes of the person speaking to him, revert in their crisis to the primitive yet highly practical concrete orientation of an early, pre-symbolic developmental level; and that, not infrequently, persons who later become psychotic have, in fact, suffered a rupture, a breakdown, as Winnicott would put it (1974), at this level (Daniel's dramatic story is axiomatic in this respect) and, therefore, when pushed close to or beyond their limits, as typically occurs during adolescence, they will regress to this level and thus suffer a partial loss of the higher ability to recognize and use metaphors and symbols as such.

It is obvious that the *older* child who plays symbolic games (using toys and role-playing) has taken an important step in the maturation process, and the child who is not able to do this is missing something essential. What is missing, namely, is practice in putting the inner world and the external world into relationship with one another (see Caper, 1999, p. 85). By engaging in healthy symbolic play, the child sets his/her internal reality into relationship with external reality: (a) by externalizing and personifying his/her internal fantasies on the toy or on his/her playmate and thereby discovering the limits of his/her own omnipotence; and (b) by exploring how the object, the "other", works internally by means of his/her own realistic projections. These phenomena were described by Freud as early as 1920 in "Beyond the pleasure principle" and by Klein in connection with her notion of the "character" (1929, 1930) and then later by Milner (1952). The toy used in symbolic play is so wonderful because it is so pliant and yet so resilient. By pliant I mean that it can accommodate so many different projections: a piece of wood can be a horse, or a gun, or a baby. But it nevertheless retains its own concrete, objective reality—after the game is over it can go back to being just a plain piece of wood. This is the bridge to the example of the rose and the adult that I discussed above. When a child plays with a companion or is fascinated by a wind-up toy, or when he/she tests to see how much maltreatment his/her doll will take, he/she is, in the words of Caper, "exploring the state of mind" of the other (1999, p. 86) (the "other" may be animate or inanimate), by gauging his/her own projections. Wanting to know, i.e., epistemophilia, is, according to Klein and Bion, essentially related to the striving to enter the body and mind of the mother, violently, exploratively, or in the search for protection and warmth, but, always, in a symbolic fashion.[15] This reminds us of Daniel, who constantly complains about not being able to get below the surface of matters, who cannot "penetrate or explore problems in depth", cannot "be absorbed in a thought", or the nurse (who also never played with dolls), who sometimes was quite incapable of grasping my state of mind.

When the force of fear and of wishes is too great, however, the game playing ceases. To dare to play, explore, experiment, and penetrate into things, whether as a child or as an adult, one has to be able to distinguish between the symbol and the symbolized, just as the distinction between the self and the absent symbolized object must be upheld. During play we learn that we can, indeed, have an effect on our objects, though, alas, only within limits. We are only able to play *after* this fact—hard and comforting as it is at the same time—has been learned at an early stage, through our *early* experience with concrete, sensorimotor reality, and if this truth has not been jeopardized by terrible inner turmoil. Only if we have learned to accept our separateness and our limits at an early age can we engage later in symbolic play. Only then are we able to form symbols and only then can symbolic representations later help us to better understand the world interactively and negotiate with reality. These are qualities that the person who later becomes psychotic would seem to be lacking—for example, children like Daniel who are "uncompromising" or, in other words, are not able to play normally.

What causes development to miscarry in this way? We may suppose that the fact that Daniel lived three months of his infancy isolated in a glass incubator, constantly plagued by pain, and, according to doctors, spent at least two nights on the verge of death, and that during this time his mother could not hold him in her arms and everyone who touched him did so wearing rubber gloves must play a role. But how?

Trauma and the fear of annihiliation

In my own psychoanalytic socialization I experienced the time when one spoke of the "schizophrenogenic mother", an unfortunate term coined by the otherwise admirable Fromm-Reichmann (Hartwell, 1996), and, during my internships, I even tended to regard the visiting mothers as if they must be this type of mother. Later, I realized the mercilessness of this view and, by seeking to overcome a simple "biographism", I learned to respect the power of internal objects and of defence and to conceptualize my experience in these terms. Working with psychotic patients, one encounters time and again difficult, if not catastrophic, anamnestic conditions—you cannot overlook or forget them. However, I learned to treat the images of the patient's past, of the character of the parents etc., as pastiches, which are composed of objective data plus the fantasies I develop in the countertransference, as a narrative that *I* need for my own therapeutic reverie to maintain a whole picture of the fragmented patient. I also learned that seriously disturbed patients, in particular, should not be offered genetic interpretations.

However, in the course of my therapeutic relationship with Daniel and in the preparation of this chapter, I have discovered innumerable references in the literature claiming that underlying that which has been termed the fear of annihiliation (Klein, 1946), primitive agony (Winnicott, 1974), aphanisis (Jones, 1927), the black hole (Grotstein, 1990; Tustin, 1972), the abject (Kristeva, 1982), white psychosis and negative hallucinosis (Green, 1975), are often traumatic events of massive proportion (see Freud, 1926d; Hopper, 1991; Jones, 1927; Tustin, 1981b).

Giovacchini observes, for example, that "intrusiveness, abandonment and even brutality are often dominant qualities of the infantile milieu" (1997, p. 36) and Boyer notes,

> There is ample evidence that the development of . . . [psychotic and borderline personality disorder] . . . results from continuous minor

> psychological assaults . . . I have found with startling regularity that in borderline and schizophrenic patients, actual dramatic psychological and/or physical sexual assaults have been commonplace rather than exceptional. [1978, p. 65]

In an outstanding article published posthumously, Winnicott writes in a similar vein

> It is wrong to think that psychotic illness is a breakdown, it is a defence organisation against a primitive agony . . . The underlying agony is unthinkable . . . [it] is *the fear of a breakdown that has already been experienced*. [1974, p. 103]

It is "unthinkable" since it cannot be expressed symbolically in neurotic terms because it came into being during a preconceptional phase of development. He outlines the consequences for therapy: "There are moments, according to my experience, when a patient needs to be told that the breakdown, a fear of which destroys his or her life, *has already been*" (*ibid.*]

The fear of annihilation and death

Encountering psychotic patients, especially at the beginning of their illness, one frequently witnesses an elementary, overwhelming panic arising from a sensation that they are falling apart (often experienced quite physically). The sensation of the "self" as a coherent, continuous entity with its ego functions is lost. Before the patient sinks too far into the illness the remaining healthy part is able to say, "I am going mad". Many psychotics speak in concrete terms of "falling" or being hurled out into the dark universe, of black holes, of non-being, of dissolution, of being dead. In general, death plays a central role in the experience of psychotic loss of identity. Sometimes parts of the body are experienced as being dead, thoughts or emotions are dead, objects go frozen stiff.

Once one has entered this world of annihilation, loneliness, and surreal alienation that is the world of the psychotic, concepts that are otherwise so helpful, such as "projective identification", "splitting", "malignant envy", etc., seem to be wanting.

It seems to me, in line with Winnicott, as if these states, with all their concrete imagery, are deferred versions of something very early, very existential. Daniel's agony in the incubator would be a paradigm of this, though admittedly an extreme one. It is the experience of absolute helplessness and failed dependency, following from catastrophic loss (Freud, 1926d); (Jones, 1927); (Tustin, 1981b) impingement (Winnicott, 1974); inadequate containment (Bion, 1962b); and breaks in holding and attachment relationships (Bick, 1968) (Hopper, 1991, p. 607) and all of this at a point in time at which the ego and the holding environment are not yet clearly differentiated from one another. As Hopper so aptly puts it, it is a period of "two brains but one mind" (*ibid.*, p. 608). It may be assumed that during this phase, i.e., before clear representations of the self and the other have become established, the loss of the other is experienced as a loss of the self (Bick, 1968; Bowlby, 1953; Tustin, 1981; Winnicott, 1974).[16] Such a loss does not cast a shadow of the object over the self; to a certain extent, the object *is* the self. In this view, it is not destructivity that would represent the "big bang" in life, but rather the experience of dying, the imminence of nothingness.

Back to Daniel

Drawing on a brief sketch of Daniel's symptomatology and anamnesis, we have so far addressed the following structural questions: what were the stressful conditions that prevented Daniel's ego boundaries, i.e., the differentiation between self and object, inside and outside, from growing properly into a solid, durable "psychic skin"? In what manner were the ego functions that now manifest a disturbance, e.g., the ability to symbolize, impaired in their basic structure early in development?

I hypothesized that, through the early forceful abandonment by an object that is as yet not really separate from the infant self:

(a) the inner representation of the so-called "good object" or, in other words, the "background presence of primary identification" (Grotstein, 1990) cannot be properly established. The latter concept is particularly helpful as it refers at once to a precursor and to the condition of development of the good object; it is an integrating object from the time in which mother and child (in the sensorimotor phase), united by the strong identification of the mother and the neediness of the child, could be said to share *one* common psychic "skin".[17] Only from this object, which comes into being through primary identification, can an idealized "good object" eventually develop through a process of *gradual* separation. In my opinion, the good internal object that should have evolved through a good separation process bears a serious defect left by the traumatic separation, and it is this that handicaps the patient's trust in himself and his creativity and robs him of his ability to be by himself and his courage to delve into the world of objects, whether of sexual or non-sexual nature. Daniel repeatedly says, "I can't really explore, penetrate a problem; I can only imitate things or, at best, pick up a thread and develop it a bit further." It is obvious what a serious liability that represents, particularly during adolescence;

(b) the unbearableness of the radical abandonment and the separation and the nothingness in its wake caused Daniel to make his burning skin, the phlegmon, which was the only perceivable companion left to him, the "subjective object", a "second skin", literally the second skin of which Bick (1968), Meltzer (1975) and Anzieu (1985) speak metaphorically. I believe the burning, painful, but at least constantly present pyodermia of then is now represented in the concrete figure of Daniel's sadistic but faithful opponent–companion: "I'm like an animal in a wire cage". Again, we recognize it in the "armour". It was this substitute skin from which Daniel could not separate himself as one typically should gradually separate from the mother's skin, because this skin is the last bastion of Daniel's self, which is threatened from inside by annihilation, by freezing. Since it is *always* present with Daniel, it cannot be symbolized: it is concrete, as a quasi-hallucination, always with him. Typically, his mother's "symbiotic" attitude later—perhaps attempting to make up for the early separation—could not mend this early damage. On the contrary, one may hypothesize that the intense, non-verbal communication ("we understood one another without words"), at a time when words should gain power in regulating nearness and distance, had a rather hampering effect on formation of a separate identity, not only—as was seen much later—on the resolution of the oedipal conflict;

(c) the defect in the integrating "background presence" (Grotstein, 1990) is what hampers an integrated experience of the self, individual body parts, elements of the psychic apparatus, thinking, feeling, and perception,[18] at least during very challenging periods of life.

Adolescence

Such a period is adolescence, which may be the phase of life that exerts the greatest strain on psychic structures, as we all know. As so aptly described by Laufer and Laufer (1984), to be an adolescent means having to cope with infantile problems in a new, largely unknown, sexually mature body with all its destructive and reproductive potential. And sexuality requires a special playful skill in the perception of and loosening of ego boundaries. It requires a certainty that even aggressive penetration does not mean final destruction of the other or the self. Good sexuality may involve experiences that are associated with a form of death, yet it is not death. Issues are involved here that we addressed when discussing symbolic play. Even so-called normal adolescents facing the exigencies of all this and more tend to go "a bit psychotic"—projections, primitive idealization and demonization, omnipotence, grandiosity, a sense of futility, hypochondria, distorted body perceptions, uncanniness, depersonalization, identity diffusion in peer groups, concentration impairment, and other more specific thought disorders are common experiences. According to Piaget, adolescence is also the stage where "formal operations" are acquired. "Discursive" formal operations require an abstract attitude, because only in abstract terms can we think about

> The non-present and the hypothetical: the past, the future, the possible, the impossible . . . [It is the time when the youngster starts] entertaining a relativity of perspectives in which it is taken

> for granted that the world would look differently if one was standing in somebody else's shoes ... [there is] a transformation from a uniperspective universe to a multiperspective one. [Josephs, 1989, p. 489]

Thus, the adolescent learns that negotiating between two reference systems is only made possible through the ambiguity of the symbolic order. Not until this stage of development does one really acquire the ability to interpret symbols. Not until one has grasped the relativity of perspectives can one understand the relativity of the meaning of words and actions. This is also the first time art can be appreciated deeply, not only in its mimetic forms.

Knowing Daniel's history, which, although unusually dramatic, I wish to emphasize seems paradigmatic for many of the psychotic adolescents I know, we can better understand what an extreme challenge this developmental phase must represent to him.[19] How is Daniel to find his bearings in life? How is he to transform the image of the mother into the image of a girl if he cannot properly symbolize the mother? How is he to fall "madly" in love, with all the projections and merging this entails, and still perceive the object in its reality as separate, as "another"? How is he to suffer abandonment without the threat of total breakdown? Into what "self" can he retire after merging in mental and physical intercourse? What hypothetical pictures of his own future can he construct? Daniel is not different in this respect from other psychotic adolescents I have worked with. Few have been able to fantasize about themselves as thirty-year-olds, for instance. Healthy adolescents can easily imagine themselves in a variety of changing, sometimes contradictory, roles—girls can dream about being a nun in the morning, a novelist in the afternoon, and a film star by evening. They do this by trial identifications on the secure basis of a "background presence of primary identification". For development to proceed, an inner psychic space is needed that is filled and warm and well ventilated, filled with "good enough" memories of an early "self-being-with-other", with fairly positive self-representations[20] and whole, flexible, good objects that can be symbolized, given up, and be mourned. Without these resources, psychotic or near-psychotic youths are left trapped in the often hated, protective inner and outer structures of their childhood.

Psychotherapy

Contrary to widespread belief, even within the psychoanalytic world, it has been my experience that the psychotic adolescent is a very fine partner in the analytic encounter. Elsewhere I have argued that even the delusional transference of the adolescent may be regarded as the potential "melting pot" of the psychosis (Pestalozzi, 1996, 1999). The relationship between psychotic material and the vital issues with which adolescence confronts all of us is often barely coded and is affectively and cognitively easy to follow. The phase of adolescence is the last time in a person's life allowing some scope for psychotic acting out, in particular within psychotherapy, and some measure of acting out—as long as it is not too dangerous to the patient or to others—is neither avoidable nor is it to be discouraged. I have come to agree with Ekstein (1976), who maintains that "psychotic acting out may become the royal road toward the strengthening of reality testing and the secondary process rather than be the primrose path to disaster" (quoted by Boyer, 1978, p. 66). In the early stages of therapy, carefully administered psychopharmaca can be an important aid. I normally see patients two to three times per week for a period of three to five years, in a face-to-face setting.[21] Occasional additional therapy sessions and telephone calls are part of this setting. With this approach, most psychotic adolescents have a very good prognosis, and they eventually go on to live a creative adult life much enriched by the experience they made on their journey through the purgatory that psychotic experience represents.

Here, I wish to further address the therapeutic consequences of only one particular aspect of the subject matter at hand: the therapeutic response to the patient's impaired ability to symbolize. I am aware that with this restriction a rich texture of transference–countertransference processes has to be neglected, which will be material for another paper.

I rely heavily on the work of Benedetti[22] and Searles, for both of whom the idea of "therapeutic symbiosis"—in the sense of "slipping into" the patient's autistic shell and allowing fusional experiences (which, of course, have to be reflected upon)—is central. Searles says,

> It is as though the patient—and analogously, the healthy young child—must first become assured of his ability to make contact with

> the therapist (or the parent) at the more primitive levels of relatedness before he can face a greater sense of apartness which must be braved, in successive degrees of intensity, in attaining successively *abstract modes of thought* and interpersonal relatedness. [1968, p. 576, my italics]

Thus, in the Kleinian tradition, Searles assumes an intermixing of self–object differentiation on the one hand and symbolic–abstract attitude on the other.

Searles refers to Piaget's three levels of cognitive development: (a) "sensorimotor" (egocentric) in infancy; (b) representational (the early stages of symbolization) in later childhood; and (c) symbolic–formal in adolescence (*ibid.*, pp. 575–579). He emphasizes that "the deeply regressed patient must establish a reasonably satisfactory mode of relatedness with the therapist (and with other people) at each successive level, before the next level can be attained' (pp. 575–576). Therapeutic symbiosis as understood by Searles, Boyer, and Benedetti also means identifying with the patient at each of these three levels.

1. An example of a type of sensorimotor intimacy (which I neither experience nor do I seek in the treatment of neurotic patients) is the episode with Daniel's backpack mentioned earlier. Not until Daniel began rummaging in his backpack did I notice that I had similarly brought my backpack into the office without any due cause. With another psychotic patient, both our feet frequently went to sleep at the same time—something that happens to me very rarely.[23] Many examples could be provided here.[24] In any case, with this level as a basis, the next level, that of concrete verbal communication, can unfold.
2. Everything that we have said thus far about the significance of concrete thinking as the last foothold and mainstay in the darkness of psychotic breakdown is of consequence for the therapeutic approach. Symbols require, by their very essence, interpretation; the concrete does not. When Daniel spoke of the hole in his head, for example, I replied, "Then we both have to make sure that I don't intrude too far with my words, and you have to help me to keep this from happening." He immediately reached for a spot on his head and said, "Yes, I'm going

to try. I think I'll be able to tell if it happens." It is crucial to remain extremely near to the images of the regressed patient and to try to enrich these with images—not with pictorial explanations of theory, but with the actual images that arise in us out of our closeness with the patient. This is one of the key elements of Benedetti's technique of "interpretation", which is not interpretation in the usual sense (i.e., uncovering latent meaning), but an enrichment of the patient's own images (which are like hostile, toxic "things" for him) with the images that emerge from the unconscious of the therapist identifying with the patient.[25] When I talk with Daniel about his "opponent" or himself as the victim, I adopt an attitude of concretization in my own perception that may even exceed his own in degree. Together with me, Daniel has been able to put himself on the side of the concrete victim, which has been an extremely valuable therapeutic step. Only from this stance has he been able to recognize his "victim" self, as a *feeling* being. If we want to try to accompany the psychotic patient out of madness—out of an inner life replete with reified persecutory objects, where words have been transformed into things—back into a world of sanity, and to restore language to its role as a means of communicating meaning, then we must first be prepared to submerge ourselves with the patient in the world of the concrete and concrete language. The patient must experience that he/she can make him/herself understood, at least in the literal sense. This can only happen if *we* acknowledge the psychic survival value of this type of communication as a regression in the service of the ego, and make it our own, at least for a time.[26] It is, in my opinion, a technical mistake to "interpret away" this last stronghold of the patient. Just as we would never say "that doesn't mean anything", we should restrain ourselves from saying "that means *x*, *y*, *z*", which *may* be appropriate when working with neurotic patients. But, when a patient finds him/herself in the discourse of "symbolic equation", he/she is simply not capable of understanding what "it means" really means; nor is he/she able to perceive the hypothetical character of any interpretation or the space, the "interval" between the interpreter and him/herself. For this reason, the psychotic patient often experiences our interpretations as a "thing", a sexual or aggressive act or a confirmation of his/her or our autism. I agree with Josephs, who doubts if it is helpful to respond to the psychotic's concrete language with the not less concretistic and sometimes equally bizarre language of the early Kleinians. When words have been transformed into things, when they have lost their power to integrate, "enlarge perspective, and expand awareness", "simply giving names to bad objects or labelling nameless dreads will do nothing to alter the nature of the underlying experience" (Josephs, 1989, pp. 492–493). When, for example, Bion responds to a schizophrenic patient who has just picked a tiny piece of skin from his face and then complains of feeling quite empty by saying, "The tiny piece of skin *is* your penis, which you have torn out and all your insides have come with it" (1953, p. 28), he is replacing discourse about the skin with discourse about the penis. As appropriate as such an interpretation may seem to us, it is questionable whether the psychotic patient, in whom symbol formation is so deeply impaired, will be capable of making the metaphoric leap from skin to penis and from emptiness to torn-out viscera, thereby decoding and integrating the complex symbolic meaning of such an interpretation (see Josephs, 1989, pp. 493–494).

3. The step out of the secure boundaries provided by the symptom of concretization into the genuinely symbolic–metaphorical realm is a big and painful one, and to be successful it has to be accompanied by a great deal of mourning. In my experience this step is taken parallel to the patient's growing ability to perceive the therapist as a person with his/her own reference system and own real limits.[27] Thus, we have arrived back at our initial hypothesis: an impaired capacity for self–object differentiation and the phenomenon of concretization are closely related to one another. Once again, let us consider Daniel, who for months at a time would often finish my thoughts for me, as if he were spinning the threads of my thoughts further in order to weave himself a new wrapping to take the place of his burning skin. Admittedly, this was still an autistic cocoon, but it provided a means to the therapist of carefully entering this autistic universe, enlarging it, subversively, by introducing her own perspectives—a situation that

> Searles and Benedetti would refer to as a "therapeutic symbiosis". This was therefore a very beneficial stage, but also one that needed to be overcome. At this time, Daniel's main occupation at home was copying simple pictures while sunk in a meditative state. He claimed that this did him a lot of good. This was clear instance of "the concrete attitude", pre-symbolic in its essence—an object that was present was copied, in contrast to the use of a symbol, which re-presents (using fantasy, ambiguity or a piece of personal interpretation) an object that is not present, or an interaction. It was disturbing to witness this behaviour in a person who had once been such a talented, creative artist. After approximately six months of intensive therapy, Daniel commented in a friendly, teasing way about one of my apparently stereotypical remarks, "I knew that you were going to say that now". This use of playful sarcasm made it clear to me that at that very moment Daniel had perceived me as an object whole and separate from himself. Not coincidentally, about this time he began writing literary texts (very good ones!) in which he was able to describe his inner situation with the conscious use of symbolism for artistic purposes. This important step was followed by many others in the therapy.

For a therapeutic symbiosis to be established, and for it to then be grown out of, it takes two people and a theory if the therapeutic encounter is not to turn into a *folie-à-deux*. The mutual manoeuvring of therapist and patient to "hatch out" of the protective shell of the therapy in a series of small steps and to detach from each other is difficult and, as in a normal maturation process, rapprochement-like crises are to be expected. This is the stage where acting out is not uncommon. There is disappointment as the "symbiosis" dissolves and omnipotence is given up.

The patient must renounce the omnipotence of having the analyst all to him/herself or being able to control his/her thoughts totally. The patient must also let go of the idea that the analyst is omnipotent in his/her ability to understand everything and protect the patient from the pains of life, which, indeed, the patient may suffer more than others. These are the painful and frequently dramatic maturational steps that lead the psychotic adolescent from the lap of psychoanalytic psychotherapy into a neurotic adult life.

And, indeed, they require symmetrical steps on the part of the analyst, too. I use the metaphor of birth because it often becomes significant during the concluding phase of this kind of therapy. Bleger has convincingly shown that the "frame" of every psychoanalytic therapy, even an "ideally kept frame" (referring to analysis with neurotic patients), also symbolizes the patient's "most primitive fusion with the mother's body and that the psychoanalyst's frame must help to re-establish the original symbiosis in order to change it". But, it is equally essential that the frame be analysed, for the "de-symbiotisation of the analyst–patient relationship is only reached with the systematic analysis of the frame at the right moment' (Bleger, 1967, pp. 515–516).

Because psychoanalytic work with seriously regressed adolescent patients can be so disturbing and may tempt the therapist with great force into acting in, it requires a particularly careful analysis of the countertransference, a rather fearless look at one's own psychotic defences and good access to supervision. We have to recognize that the "therapeutic frame" or "containing", so crucial in the therapeutic setting we devise and so meaningful in the realm of our theory, not only represents the mother's womb or father's forbidding authority to the patient, but also to ourselves.

Notes

1. The editors thank the Editorial Board of the *International Journal of Psychoanalysis* for its permission to publish this paper, first published in 2003 in the *International Journal of Psychoanalysis, 84*: 733–753.
2. Parts of this paper were presented on 19 April 2000 at the 47th annual meeting of the Verein für Analytische Kinder und Jugendpsychoanalyse, other parts to the 4th Conference of the Child and Adolescent Section of the EFPP in Caen in September 2001, and were published in honour of the eightieth birthday of my teacher, Gaetano Benedetti.
3. I do not strictly differentiate here between the *rhetorical* meaning of the words "metaphor" and "symbol". Both are used in very different ways that sometimes overlap in modern linguistic and semiotics and in psychoanalysis—by Freud himself, both before and after he wrote *The Interpretation of Dreams* (see Schmid Noerr, 2000, p. 465), by Lacan, in particular, and by the modern classical thinkers in the field of symbolic

theory (Cassirer, 1923, 1924, 1929; Langer, 1942; and, in some respects, Lorenzer, 1970). Modern linguistics describes the differences as being gradual (see Kurz, 1997, p.73). Common to both are the rhetorical forms of synecdoche (*pars pro toto* and vice versa) and analogy. In both cases something stands for something else and highlights it at the same time (i.e. they are substitutive). A symbol, whether an actual object or a verbal expression, can in all forms of culture refer to something "unspeakable" (the transcendental element within religions, or the unconscious in the psychoanalytical view). In contrast to symbols, "with metaphors . . . our attention is focused more on the words themselves and on semantic compatibilities and incompatibilities. With symbols, our attention is focused more on the experience that is being represented . . . Metaphors activate a consciousness of language, and symbols a consciousness of things" (Kurz, 1997, p. 73). This is especially true when the metaphor is new and not yet worn out. Within language, verbal symbols are thus more like what Langer described as "presentative symbolisation" rather than "discursive symbolisation". The latter two forms of symbolization will be relevant to arguments formulated in a later part of this paper.

4. Searles even says, "The mutual sharing of such metaphorical experience would seem to be as intimate a psychological contact as adult human beings can have with one another" (1968, p. 583).
5. Segal's examples of the "stool" and the violin ("I can't masturbate in public with my violin"), upon which her concept of the "symbolic equation" is based, are well known. For the psychotic person, in contrast to the neurotic, the violin is not an *as if* penis, it *is* a penis (Segal, 1957, pp. 38–39). Likewise, the analyst's sexual interpretation is not understood as an interpretation, but is perceived as an *act* of seduction or castration, as Winnicott (1947), Balint (1968) and others have reported.
6. One may ask, what are the conditions in the transference–countertransference development that enable the development of such "feelings", where previously the psychotic devastation had seemingly destroyed the ability to feel—at least in a conscious manner? I suppose that what happened between Daniel and me can best be described by Bion's notion of containment. Probably *Ucs.* projective–introjective communications allowed me to experience Daniel's communications as truly meaningful, e.g., I could give meaning to his concrete armour as a protection, which would be different from interpreting it as a defence. (Looking back to "our beginnings" he told me years later that this was the crucial moment that made him decide on a "talking cure".) This

helped us to share a meaning, to restore again and again alpha function and to consider me or our sessions as the place to restore links between objects, between sensations and feelings. It is more the atmosphere where all communications are potentially meaningful and the hope that these feelings can one day be felt, sustained, and mourned and, further, the narcissistic upgrading of a patient in states of utter loss of self-esteem, just through becoming meaningful in the eyes of the other, that helps emerging from that utter lostness that psychotic experience frequently entails. Daniel often asked me if I thought his desperate state would ever get better. I sometimes answered that I did think so (which I actually did), but I always added that my hope was not "my" hope but his at the moment unfelt hope, which a healthy part of him, through unknown channels (and I meant projective identification), must have deposited in me. And so I do think that we will manage and one day he will rightly claim back his part. When a "hope", a "good part", is being split off into the analyst, it is crucial, too, that this "projection" be made again and again comprehensible to the patient (he/she must be given a receipt for his/her deposit in me), otherwise it would mean a depletion, an impoverishment of the patient's self.

7. Except in connection with women who later develop a so-called "obligatory [true] homosexuality" (i.e., a form of female homosexuality relating to an early developmental disturbance) (see Dorpat, 1990, p. 123).
8. This was intimated by Freud (1900a) in his theory of thing and word presentation. He hypothesized that the concrete thinking observed in patients suffering from schizophrenia, which at that time was known as dementia praecox, is directly related to "thing presentation" and thus to the primary process.
9. "Depending on the context or situation, the sentence *Peter is a child* may be understood literally (if Peter is six years old, for instance, or metaphorically, if Peter is 30 years old)" (Kurz, 1997, pp. 13–14).
10. In this passage I rely heavily on reflections of Caper (1999, pp. 84–94).
11. Orientation in this respect may also be lost in cases of extreme psychotrauma when our basic trust in the reliability, i.e., understandability, of the world breaks down.
12. I am much indebted to Anne Alvarez, who made me use the word proto-symbolic instead of pre-symbolic as in an earlier version of this paper by saying that "babies, when they are studying thoughtfully the pattern of light and shade, or say, the blueness of a blue curtain, or the

mother's present but mobile and therefore interesting face, are getting alpha function around the experience or thought, and making it thinkable, and that is the beginning of symbolization, and such moments occur from day one, and are not purely bodily" (personal communication).

13. Corresponding to Stern's RIGs = "Representation of Interactions that have been Generalised" (1985, p. 97).
14. Representational thinking can be "discursive" or "non-discursive", as demonstrated by Langer in her classical treatment of the subject (1942). Language, with its vocabulary and grammar, its series of independent units linked one to the other, its relationship to causality, and ever-present abstraction, is "discursive". "Presentational thinking", with its symbols that are always perceived as a whole (the elements that make up a picture are, in fact, just a collection of spots), always in close connection to the object, and, owing to the sensuousness of their nature, never far removed from the emotional realm, is "non-discursive". Music and the arts are highly developed forms of this type of symbolization, and the symbolic play of children also has its root here. Both these types of symbolism develop along parallel lines and supplement and complement each other, and there are no grounds for believing that "discursive symbolism" has *evolved from* an earlier, more primitive stage of "presentational" symbolism. Both are based on real, concrete modes of experience where the signifier and the signified are initially one and the same and only gradually come to be distinguished one from the other.
15. See also Chasseguet-Smirgel's archaic matrix of the Oedipus complex (1986).
16. The similarities and the differences to Mahler's concept of the "symbiotic phase" (Mahler, Pine, & Bergman, 1975) cannot be discussed here, but see also Gergely (2000), Pestalozzi (2000).
17. See the "we–self" of Stern, 1985, p. 101.
18. Green comments as follows on these states:

> The final result is paralysis of thought which is expressed in a negative hypochondriasis, particularly with regard to the head, i.e. a feeling of empty-headedness, of a hole in mental activity, inability to concentrate, to remember etc. The struggle against these feelings can bring in its wake an artificial thought process: ruminations, a kind of pseudo-obsessional compulsive thought . . . etc. One is tempted to think that these are only the effects of repression. But this is not so . . . they are forms of recathexis. [1975, pp. 41–42]

19. Obviously, I am arguing this with the benefit of hindsight. We know that a large number of schizophrenic breakdowns occur during adolescence and very often at the time of the person's first love affair.
20. That is, a good "sense of core-self":

> a sense of core self includes (1) *self-agency*, in the sense of authorship of one's own action and nonauthorship of the action of others . . . (2) *self-coherence* . . . (3) *self-affectivity* . . . (4) *self-history* having a sense of . . . continuity with one's past so that one "goes on being" and can even change while remaining the same. The "sense of self" is an experiential integration. This sense of core self will be the foundation for all more elaborate senses of the self to be added later.These four basic self-experiences . . . are necessary for adult psychological health. It is only in major psychosis that we see a significant absence . . . [see Stern, 1985, pp. 70–71]

21. Occasionally, usually after years with this setting, once language regains its proper function, where words are words and not "things" violently pushed into or pulled out of the patient, such patients can use the couch with benefit. Prior to this I myself need a "concrete" visual idea of what happens to the patient in response to my interventions and he/she needs to experience my presence concretely at times, when the right words are, on my part, missing.
22. Benedetti explicitly addresses this issue, primarily in his work *Psychotherapie als existentielle Herausforderung* (1992, pp. 33–44).
23. One can ask oneself, what was the countertransferential background to this fully unconscious response of mine? Remembering well the atmosphere of the first few minutes, I believe my response was twofold: identifying with a healthy part of this adolescent as if I had said, "Here we are, let's go on our tour, you with your heavy bag and I with my lighter one. I hope and trust that we will get somewhere". Indeed, this patient could project into me right at the beginning the very *hope* that he could not properly feel (which, of course, had to be interpreted to him in due course, cf. n. 5). On the contrary, he verbally expressed repeated doubts in the chances of "just talking". On a deeper level, my unconscious reaction reminds me of the regressive gesture of mothers, with which they "instinctively" imitate the facial expression of their young babies, everywhere in the world, as one of the many paths of bonding and of regulating the affective state of the child. Though this patient very much later explained to me that what kept him in therapy was that our "talking" could soon give "meaning to the meaningless" (*sic*) referring

to the armour as safety against inner threats, (cf. n. 5) I believe the mutual experience of "matching" between therapist and psychotic patient, expressed in such verbal and even unconscious messages "from unconscious to unconscious", are most importantly the stuff of which an initial working alliance (or a therapeutic impasse) is made from. Recent neurobiological evidence seems to suggest that—as long ago intuited by Bion—the pathways of such communications are fast, effective and highly motivating (De Masi, 2001, p. 77).

24. Being "in sync" like this can give the psychotic patient a wonderful feeling of oceanic attachment, but it can also be experienced as something horrible, dangerous, devouring. Careful monitoring of these scenes of interaction can become crucial for the maintenance and outcome of therapy.
25. In this "symbiosis" a certain detoxification of these images is hoped for.
26. An example of this is provided in the case of a severely psychotic patient, who had constructed a highly complex system of delusions, including male and female and positive and negative suns, a male and female moon, etc., and who, in order to bind these elements with one another, spent five days running in a circle around her table. One day, the therapist of this patient was woken up by a family member who declared that the sun was shining, and the therapist, still half asleep, asked, "Which of the suns . . .?" There is nothing mystical or sentimental about this phenomenon—it is what Benedetti describes as "counteridentification" (which is different from countertransference): "We can hypothesise that the intensive process of counteridentification in the therapist represents a form of partial regression which allows the therapist to become syntonic with his or her psychotic partner" (1983, p. 59).
27. Until then, one has to cope with a continuous cycle of over- and underestimation of the therapist by the patient and, concomitantly, with feelings of omnipotence and helplessness on the part of the therapist.

CHAPTER FOUR

Splitting of psychic bisexuality in autistic children

Didier Houzel

The meticulous application of psychoanalytic technique, together with an outstanding "capacity for reverie", enabled Frances Tustin to discover the nature of the unconscious fantasy that lies at the heart of autistic functioning and organization: that of an unbridgeable discontinuity between self and object, represented by the "broken button" of her young patient John and by the persecutory feelings of being ripped apart that practically all autistic children express in the course of their psychotherapy. Tustin summarized her findings in her description of the mouth–tongue–nipple–breast discontinuity and the concept of "premature psychological birth"—in other words, the necessity for the child to process an awareness of physical separation from the object, the maternal breast, even though, at that point in development, he or she does not yet possess the mental capacity to symbolize it.

I would like to dedicate this chapter to Frances Tustin. I know that she personally had to face up to terrible anxieties that had to be overcome in order for her to throw light on that fundamental level of human experience at which the Self, emerging from its confusion with the Object, begins to establish its basic identity. In a very moving interview I did with her, she talked of certain crucial moments in her own life, her analysis with Bion, and her discovery of the fantasy that lies at the heart of autistic spectrum disorder. The convergence of these three components was in itself striking, and from it a new light seemed to shine forth. As with any discovery in psychoanalysis, hers was made thanks to an alternating movement between her own personal analysis and her work as psychotherapist. To my mind, it is mainly thanks to that approach, which she carried out courageously and in relative isolation, that we now have a deeper understanding of autism and of the way psychotherapy can help children who suffer from it.

I shall therefore take her work as my starting point before going on to suggest some of my own hypotheses concerning the psychotherapeutic treatment of children with autism. Though it is difficult to choose exactly which topic to deal with, I shall focus on that part of her work that involves what I call the "pathology of otherness" and the link between that pathology and primary defects in the integration of psychic bisexuality. In her book *Autistic States in Children*, Tustin (1981b) makes a clear link between these two fundamental aspects of her discoveries. Let me give two extracts to illustrate my point:

> In rare states of occasional awareness of bodily separateness, there is a soft "me" and a hard "not-me", which threatens to hurt their soft vulnerability. In order to shut out this hard "not-me", "me" and "not-me" are partitioned off from each other and kept rigidly apart . . . [*ibid.*, p. 61]

> Gradually, soft sensations become associated with "taking-in", with receptivity, "hard" sensations become associated with "entering" and "thrusting". At some point, these become associated with the infant's bisexuality. "Hard" thrusting becomes "male", and "soft" receptivity becomes "female". When, on the basis of a co-operative suckling experience, the "hard" entering nipple and tongue are experienced as working together with the "soft" receptive mouth and breast, then a "marriage" between "male" and "female" elements takes place. [*ibid.*, p. 84]

Thus, the combined nipple–breast object is bisexual, the masculine component being represented by the nipple and the feminine one by the breast. If it proves impossible to integrate these two components into a harmonious and co-operative whole, the outcome would seem to be that particular kind of pathology of otherness we call autism: on the one hand the combined object is split into its masculine and feminine components, and on the other there is absolute separation between self, experienced as soft and vulnerable, and not-self, felt to be hard and threatening. It seems to me, however, that we still have to understand how these two dimensions connect together: feminine and masculine on the one hand, and self and not-self on the other. In order to do this, we have to explore the dynamic processes that underpin fantasy representations. This approach seems crucial to me not only from a theoretical point of view but also at the technical level, since only interpretations that have their source in the intimate dynamics of our own minds have any chance of being helpful. As Alvarez (1992) points out, we have to be active in making contact with the more or less closed mental world of our young patients; in order to do this, we must first understand how their minds work and how their internal dynamics tend to bring about this kind of mental closure.

I would like to emphasize the point that, in Frances Tustin's description, the source of autistic anxiety does not lie, as is often stated, in the fact that child and mother are separate, but in what Tustin called "awareness of bodily separateness" (Tustin, 1981b, p. 11)—in other words, awareness of a gap between self and object. This gap is not simply geographical as in the experience of separation, it is also temporal, i.e., it causes the self to experience frustration and delay between the arousal of a drive-orientated impulse and subsequent satisfaction. Above all, it is dynamic: the object is neither continuous with the self, nor is it under the self's control. As a result, a gradient of psychic energy is created, just as when a mountain stream takes a sudden downward plunge, accelerating its otherwise moderate descent; in the ensuing waterfall, a considerable amount of energy is liberated. Such a gradient can be overcome only if the child's mind is able to construct some kind of representation and symbolization, thereby enhancing the creation of structurally stable forms within that dynamic system. Frances Tustin's "premature psychological birth" is a traumatic state in which the child is faced with an unbridgeable dynamic gap between self and object; the object, however, is not unresponsive to the self, as a somewhat superficial reading would have us believe—on the contrary, the self is attracted to the object in so powerful a manner that it cannot help being dragged into uncontrollable and destructive undercurrents. I would suggest that autistic defences aim to protect the self against such a fate, but at the cost of a total lack of communication with others—in order to suppress the insurmountable gradient, the object's very existence has to be denied, thereby compromising any possibility of psychic development, since this, too, requires a relationship in order to thrive.

Frances Tustin's discoveries are at the opposite end of the spectrum from the deficit hypotheses put forward by cognitivist writers: lack of a theory of mind (Baron-Cohen, Leslie, & Frith, 1985), deficiencies in perception and expression of emotional communication (Hobson, 1991). There may indeed be a defect somewhere, but it is secondary and not primary—the result of a defensive process aiming not to fill up some insufficiency but to neutralize an overflow: that of drive-orientated energy or of emotional turmoil. We see this overflow at work when, in therapy, the child begins to emerge from the autistic shell that served as a protection against awareness of the outside world—and hence of the pain that being separate entails.

This was the case with Frances Tustin's patient John, who, in the now-famous 360th session (Tustin, 1972, pp. 15–16), expressed the fantasy of the "black hole with the nasty prick"; thanks to this fantasy, the therapist was able to grasp the nature of the anxieties against which John was trying to defend himself. Here the overflow was in the form of a "rocket" or a "firework breast", something explosive that shot out of the mouth and breast—in other words in the gap that separated self from object.

"Alan" was an autistic boy I began treating when he was four years old (he is now sixteen); in his case, the overflow was also expressed as fireworks. That material appeared in a session some two and a half years into the therapy, which at that point was being carried out on a four times per week basis. There had been a partial interruption of the therapy lasting one year, since I had moved to another part of my country; I was at that time able to offer Alan only two sessions a month, travelling back to my former home town on that basis to continue the treatment. One year before the session I shall now report, Alan's family also moved to the town where I was working in order for the therapy to get back on to a much more sustainable footing. The session took place shortly after the summer vacation, and just before a scheduled session that had had to be cancelled. Some sessions previously, Alan, to my surprise, had asked: "How do you get ready for being born?" I of course understood the question to mean being born psychically. It was only later that I realized that, for a child coming out of autism, that kind of birth was inevitably explosive.

29 September 1993

Alan talked about dodgem cars and a funfair that he called "the pig fair"; his mother had taken him there, telling him there would be dodgems, but there weren't any. He had been very angry about that. He said this over and over again; I finally associated to my absence the next day and to the fact that we had had to cancel the scheduled session—I said that he was no doubt very disappointed that the session was not going to take place and that it made him feel very angry, just like when he saw there were no dodgems. I had the impression that this interpretation evoked claustrophobic anxiety in him—he asked me the time, then at what time the session ended, and he came up to me to check my watch. I said that perhaps he wanted to push inside me like a dodgem could; that way, he wouldn't have to feel separated because of my absence—but then, of course, he might be afraid that he would be imprisoned inside me without ever being able to get out.

At that point, a new kind of material appeared. He sucked up some water straight from the basin that, as usual, I had prepared for him, then spat it all out on the floor, saying that he was making a fireworks display. He did this several times. I interpreted that he felt the session to be like sucking up mummy–Houzel's milk and that he represented this through his sucking up of the water in the basin; I added that he experienced my absence the following day as a bad breast-feed that caused him to feel some very powerful things in his mouth, like exploding fireworks for example.

He then spat out some water several times, saying: "Who have I killed?" He spoke of gunpowder, cannons, cannon-balls—but they were supposed to be quite far away, somewhere outside the therapy room: "Where is the cannon-ball?" "It's over there," he said. "Where is the gunpowder?" "It's over there," he added, pointing out of the window to somewhere in the distance. I said he was putting all

> the dangerous things very far away, so that they might be less of a threat. Alan then spoke of how dirty all that kind of thing could be and how it would have to be cleaned up. I replied that perhaps he was not only very angry about the fact that I was not going to be here for him the following day but also very worried in case his anger might transform the good milk into something dirty that would have to be cleaned up.
>
> Again he mentioned the end of the session. I interpreted that maybe he was feeling something to do with a breast-feed that was coming to a close. He then spoke of his little sister's ears (she was still a baby at this point), saying that they were like little bells and that he wanted to clean them. I replied that his anger probably plugged his own baby-ears, so that, not being able to hear what other people were saying to him, he couldn't communicate with them—maybe that was why they had to be cleaned.

The powerful explosive energy that is liberated when children emerge from their autistic state must be both contained and transformed in order for it to be used in the service of representation and symbolization. The "cluster of sensations" that the "mouth-encircled nipple", as Frances Tustin put it (1981b, p. 132), evokes in the child has two possible outcomes: either it explodes like a rocket-cum-fireworks display at the end of the feed, i.e., when the infant is obliged to recognize that nipple–breast and mouth are in fact separable, or it is transformed into a trace of the infant's encounter with the object, a trace internalized within the infant's mind as a structurally stable representation that other such experiences in the future will enhance. In fact, what I am describing here is quite simply the mysterious process whereby beta-elements are transformed into alpha-elements. By highlighting the idea of stability, I want to emphasize the fact that this process of transformation tends to create stability where before there was turmoil. It replaces the explosive phenomena with a stable representation of the combined nipple–breast object, thereby enabling the infant at each new encounter not only to recognize it as identical to what it was before, but also to assimilate other objects to it when new experiences are made. In this manner, the internal world is enriched and becomes more complex as links are generated between different traces of these encounters. "The finding of an object is in fact a refinding of it," wrote Freud (1905d, p. 222). To put it another way, no new encounter is possible without there first having been one in which the primary representation of an available and reliable object was created. Thereafter, each new encounter enhances and diversifies this representation, so that—to paraphrase the French poet Alfred de Musset—it is "neither entirely the same nor completely different". The autistic child, on the other hand, does not benefit from such continuity, since even though the encounter with the object may give rise to an ecstatic experience, it always ends up by being explosive and destructive.

As we know, Frances Tustin insisted on the fact that it is important for autistic children to have a regular and predictable setting, and recommended that sessions take place at the same time each day. I would add that it is necessary also for the child to have several sessions per week, especially in the initial stages of the therapy.

How, then, is turmoil transformed into stability, unpredictable into predictable, sensation into representation, and mere excitation into emotion? Bion suggested that the containing relationship could be a useful model: the raw sensory element—the "β" element—is projected into the container, where it is transformed and then returned to the infant in a form that the mind can digest.

Here again we are dealing with fantasy representations: container, contained, the relationship through which the contained penetrates the container. . . . And here again we must try to clarify the dynamics that lie beneath these representations. I have referred to the idea of structural stability as underpinning my thinking in this chapter, and I shall continue to refer to it in this context; for me, the containing object is the structurally stable part of the dynamic system created by the containing relationship. The concept of structural stability is an integral part of the theory of dynamic systems, and denotes the capacity by which such a system can generate stable forms within itself in spite of the constant movement to which all of its component parts are subjected. One example of structural stability suggested by the French mathematician René Thom (1989) is the drainage system of streams and rivers in the dynamic eco-system of the water cycle in a given region. To put it more clinically, the mother's mind must function in such a way as to represent the stable part of the dynamic relationship that is set up between her and her infant. I must, however, immediately add that this container does not consist solely of maternal elements; it must also have paternal qualities that are intimately bound up with the maternal ones. On this I am in complete agreement with Frances Tustin when she speaks of the infant's psychic bisexuality. It was in a musical way that Alan showed me the importance of integrating psychic bisexuality in the therapeutic relationship. At the end of each session I would make a sketch of the days of the week, hatching in the days when he had sessions and leaving the others empty, so that he would be able to visualize our forthcoming schedule.

Shortly after we began once again to have four sessions a week (after the year-long part-interruption that I mentioned), he copied out my diagram (Figure 1). Before this, he had only scribbled or drawn spiral shapes without any representative content.

In November 1993, a few weeks after the session I have just reported, he did a very talented imitation of an organist playing low and high notes—taken together, it was very pleasant-sounding. Alan has an fine ear for music; he is a talented pianist, and in his imitation of organ-playing, I had no difficulty in recognizing a Bach fugue. He drew on the floor a set of organ pipes and explained how, when air passed through them, musical notes came out. I encouraged him to draw them on a sheet of paper, and he agreed (Figures 2 and 3).

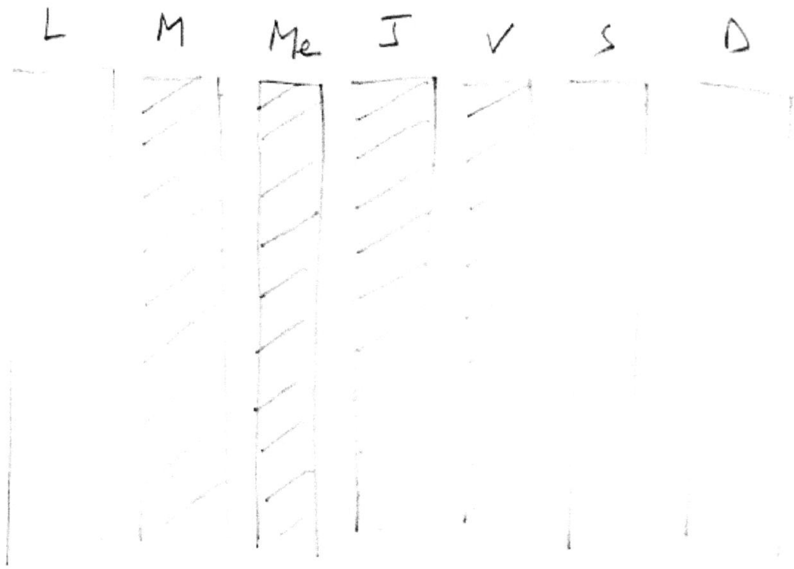

Figure 1.

Figure 2.

Figure 3.

I could then see the resemblance between these pipes and the diagram I drew of what I called "our days", which little by little were transformed into musical notes. This musical metaphor brought to mind a paper by Suzanne Maiello on "The sound envelope and primal rhythms" (Maiello, 2000). Alan seemed to be telling me that the envelope of our sessions needed to have both maternal–feminine tones (the high-pitched notes coming from the organ) and paternal–masculine ones (the low notes) in order to produce a pleasant-sounding melody that would promise him an opening on to psychic birth and on to the world as a whole. This interpretation of high-pitched and low-pitched notes was, as it were, forced on me by Alan himself, who compared the low notes made by musical instruments to the voices of the menfolk in his family and in particular to that of his paternal grandfather.

I would, however, suggest that both Bion's model of containment and Tustin's description of infant bisexuality need to be modified slightly. In his model of the containing relationship, Bion used the well-known gender symbols ♀, the feminine symbol, for the container, and ♂, the masculine one, for the contained, and combined them together thus: ♀♂. In her description of infant bisexuality, Tustin spoke of the relationship between feminine "receptivity" and masculine "penetration". In my view, there is an even more primitive level in which masculine and feminine elements are not yet in a penetrating–receptive relationship; they are more woven together into an integrated whole in which the masculine elements reinforce the feminine ones. The masculine component is there to buttress the maternal recipient to prevent its being deformed and pulled out of shape, or even torn by the sheer intensity of the infant's projections; in addition, it plays a mediating role between the infant and the object, just as the nipple comes between the greedy mouth and the breast. At this level, the integration of psychic bisexuality is based on the intricate and complementary functions of nipple and breast. Without attempting to define categories too narrowly, I would say that qualities such as receptivity and flexibility belong to the maternal–feminine side of the container, while those such as consistency and orientating belong to the paternal–masculine one. From the point of view of the mind, these correspond to the mother's maternal and paternal identifications, united in a harmonious relationship. To my way of thinking, it is essential to remember this double polarity; male or female, we all have maternal and paternal objects in our minds in a more or less harmonious relationship. The infant has thus first to process the psychic bisexuality of the container; it is on this that any possibility of integrating psychic bisexuality at the most primitive of levels depends. It was some six-and-a-half years into his therapy that Alan taught me this, as he recalled a memory from his very early childhood in which his grandfather gave support to a weakened maternal container. (Though this screen memory relates to Alan's *paternal* grandfather, he does indeed seem to have played a highly supportive role with respect to Alan's mother, making up for what had hitherto been experienced as a deficit in her psychic reality.)

3 September 1996

Alan reminded me that some time before I had warned him not to spit at me; in fact, I had once threatened to end the session if he carried on doing so. He asked question after question about what would have happened had I in fact put an end to that session: would the taxi that brings him here for his sessions have taken him back home? Would he have had to wait in the waiting-room? Then he spoke about the various occasions on which a session had had to be cancelled. After that, he mentioned the fact that, according to legend, church bells fall silent at Easter because everyone is saddened by Jesus' death; but on Easter Sunday they all come back from Rome because Jesus rises from the dead. Then he came close to me and tried to tickle me, telling me about the rotating lamps at the pig fair . . .

I replied that we felt sad every time we could not meet, like when sessions had to be cancelled or during the holiday period we had just had; maybe this was like feeling sad at Jesus's death. Then we were glad to be back together again, like when church bells begin ringing again on Easter Sunday. I added that perhaps he was trying to get rid of all the sadness by tickling me or in switching on inside me the rotating lamps he had seen at the pig fair.

Then he spoke of things he said were disgusting and not very nice. Once, when saying hello to his aunt Marie-Claire, he had smelled her armpits; his mother had smacked him for that. On another occasion he had demanded a biscuit from another of his aunts, and his mother had reprimanded him for doing so. He spoke of pony droppings, a pony that had diarrhoea; Alan soaked a sheet of paper in water to make balls representing pony droppings and threw them against the wall.

I said that all this reminded me of something his parents had told me. For professional reasons to do with his father, they had lived abroad when Alan was about one year old. He had suffered from chronic diarrhoea that had lasted eleven months, and no doctor had been able to discover the cause. I added that perhaps he was wondering whether I was going to be like a mummy thinking all that was disgusting, or on the contrary a mummy ready to accept everything that came from her little boy. Since he had spoken about bad smells, and especially about odours from armpits, I added that it was very hot in the country they had stayed in abroad, he had perspired a lot and maybe that had made a bad smell (his parents had told me that he had suffered also from a skin infection that had been attributed to excessive perspiration).

Alan went on to tell me about something that had taken place when, according to him, he was about 2½ years old. He was out sailing with Grandad in his boat, and had vomited. His mother smacked him, saying: "Why did you vomit?" Alan told me that the sea was so rough that he had felt sea-sick. He explained that he had noticed a lot of marker buoys indicating places that boats should steer clear of in case they ran aground on the rocks.

I spoke of his desire that I should be like a mummy who was both able to accept whatever came out of him without feeling disgust—diarrhoea, vomit, "not nice" things, etc.—and who had a "grand daddy" figure with her who would be able to navigate properly and prevent the boat breaking up on the rocks.

Alan listened carefully and calmly to me—in fact, I had never seen him so calm before.

I think that this session is a good illustration of how important it is for the maternal container to have the internal support of a paternal object (the "Grand-daddy") that makes it solid enough to weather any storms (the boat that did not run aground) and gives it some idea of where it is heading (grandfather's skilful manoeuvres). The death of Jesus probably refers to the mother's depression—while she was expecting Alan, her own mother had died.

There is one very important technical consequence entailed by the bisexual nature of the psychic container. Psychotherapists have to be in contact with their own parental identifications and constantly work over the links between the maternal and paternal objects that inhabit their internal world. The same person has to exemplify these double identifications and the harmonious relationship that exists between them. In other words, it is no use expecting some outside person to inject a so-called paternal element whenever the therapist has seemed to function as a "pure female element" (to use Winnicott's expression (1966, p. 173), or introduce some maternal element whenever "purely paternal" functioning has taken place. If the maternal container is dissociated from the paternal buttress, the self inevitably feels swallowed up and annihilated, and if the paternal elements are dissociated from the maternal container they are experienced as persecutory, like the "nasty prick" mentioned by Frances Tustin's patient.

The autistic process tends to make a very deep and very early split between the elements of psychic bisexuality. Therapists are therefore subjected to splitting projections that tend to dissociate the elements of their own bisexuality, hence the need for meticulous and on-going processing of the countertransference in order to reintegrate the dispersed elements of their own psychic bisexuality. The active reclaiming function that Alvarez describes in *Live Company* (Alvarez, 1992) seems to me to represent the paternal–masculine aspect of the therapist-as-container's psychic bisexuality, with transference receptivity being the maternal–feminine aspect.

The penetration relationship between masculine and feminine aspects of psychic bisexuality seems to me to constitute a second stage, i.e., after the development of part-objects in the infant's internal world and the formation of early primal-scene fantasies. I see these two levels of psychic bisexuality more in terms of logical rather than chronological priority: containing object level, and part-object level. As soon as integration becomes possible at the first of these levels, the second stage appears, and there follows an oscillation between the two, similar to that between paranoid–schizoid and depressive positions, which Bion located at the shift from part-objects to whole objects.

If, instead of penetration, there is a weaving-together of bisexual elements at this first level, what is the nature of the relationship between container and contained? Alan's psychotherapy, like that of other children with autism, tends to make me think that it is a relatively non-differentiated one, but dominated more by anal than by genital considerations, as Bion himself described:

> I shall state the theory first in terms of a model, as follows: The infant suffers pangs of hunger and fear that it is dying, wracked by guilt and anxiety, and impelled by greed, messes itself and cries. The mother picks it up, feeds it and comfort it, and eventually the infant sleeps.
>
> Reforming the model to represent the feelings of the infant we have the following version: the infant, filled with painful lumps of faeces, guilt, fears of impending death, chunks of greed, meanness and urine, evacuates these bad objects into the breast that is not there. As it does so the good object turns the no-breast (mouth) into a breast, the faeces and urine into milk, the fears of impending death and anxiety into vitality and confidence, the greed and meanness into feelings of love and generosity and the infant sucks its bad property, now translated into goodness, back again. [Bion, 1963, p. 31]

The vomit Alan splashed all over his grandfather's boat is a fantasy expression to do with projecting the pain he felt into the container, reinforced by all the diarrhoea, "not nice" things, and bad smells. One session in particular from the ninth year of the therapy was significant in that it helped me understand the process by which projections are transformed into more digestible elements.

11th February 2000

For the past two sessions, Alan had been singing the military tunes he heard his grandfather sing. He interspersed this with burps, made rude remarks and talked a lot about things that were "not nice". He caricatured his mother scolding his younger brother for burping into Uncle Gaston's ear.

When he said that his burps made the same noise as a helicon (a brass band instrument for playing military music), I interpreted this in terms of his wondering whether I would be able to help him transform his burps - along with a whole lot of other things he felt inside - into nice things like his grand-dad's military music.

He said that when the family lived abroad when he was very young, he used to be afraid of the helicon he heard when the Foreign Legion

Figure 4.

> played their music. He drew soldiers at the Arc de Triomphe playing helicons and trumpets.
>
> Then he spoke of the school year starting again in September, when the lifeguards no longer keep watch on the beaches and it becomes more dangerous to go swimming.
>
> I interpreted the beach without lifeguards in terms of a dangerous sea/mother without a father to prevent people drowning, and the helicon in terms of a deep-throated father who could be a bit frightening. I again mentioned his grandad's military music, saying that he no doubt wanted me to be like a mummy with a "Grand daddy" inside who could transform "not nice" things into nice music.

The grandfather figure came more and more into the picture in Alan's communications during the sessions. Just a few months ago, he drew the following portrait: Grandad, proud and impressive in his military uniform, is wearing a black and red necktie that seems to be coming out of his mouth, representing an indigestible part that Alan still needs to project into a bisexual container in order to be transformed.

Alan was obviously identified with his grandfather, who provided him with a powerful masculine image; but we still had

Figure 5.

work to do to process what was coming out of the grandfather's mouth like a gush of vomit in order to make it digestible.

In recent months, Alan has expressed this in terms of an excess of vibrations. He used to live next to an arsenal, and the end of each day's work was announced by the whine of a siren, always at the same hour of the day. He was frightened by the noise of this siren, which was located near a bridge over a narrow channel coming in from the sea. This description expressed the intense vibrations he had experienced as a child heralding some kind of catastrophe to do with the absence of a bisexual container that could have transformed his cries of distress into a harmonious counterpoint in which paternal low notes and maternal high-pitched ones could have come together. The bridge in Alan's drawings represents the paternal function of linking and mediating [what Resnik (1986, p. 30*n*, 1990, pp. 102, 106) calls "the paternal bridging function"], a guarantee against being swallowed up by a sea/mother that Alan described as threatening and freezing cold; I interpreted this as a representation of his mother's depression when her own mother died near the beginning of the pregnancy. At the same time, the paternal bridge appears weak and is threatening to collapse because of the sheer magnitude of the vibrations caused by the siren—in other words, the sheer forcefulness of infantile projections reactivated at puberty. However, these dangers can now be represented; they are no longer the "nameless dread" that arises when the infant's β-elements are projected without there being a container to transform them into α-elements.

I would like to conclude this paper with an extract from one of Alan's recent sessions, one that took place just before the last summer vacation. That session seems to condense into one complex and intricate relationship the three levels that psychic bisexuality has to integrate: container, part-object and whole-object. When this final level is reached, emotion replaces the excited arousal and bodily vibrations that threatened to disrupt everything that had been constructed up to that point, just like the vibrations of the siren threatened to undermine the bridge—the bridge that linked us together in the transference as well as linking Alan to his internal objects.

27th June 2001

Alan took out the drawings he had done in previous sessions and said they were "morbid". He looked carefully at one drawing in which people were falling off the bridge because the arsenal siren had made too loud a noise and the resultant vibrations had caused the bridge to collapse.

He said it was the director's fault for switching the siren turbine on too powerfully.

He then drew the bridge again, with people standing on it as the siren began to whine.

On this occasion, he drew the siren under the bridge in the shape of a circle with spokes coming out of it to represent the pipes through which the sound came out; he added a long series of exclamation points, as in comic strips, to indicate that the noise was far too loud. The people on the bridge were merely sketched out roughly, and their hearts were placed in their chests—the drawing illustrated the fact that the vibrations of the siren struck them there. Alan said that this made them feel things very powerfully. Then he added that the people were going to fall into the ice-cold sea when the bridge broke up under the

Figure 6.

Figure 7.

impact of the vibrations—it was going to be like the *Titanic* shipwreck in which a thousand people had drowned. He drew someone standing under the bridge on whose leg an enormous rock fell from the bridge. Lower down, he drew another figure who was deafened by the noise of the siren—he illustrated this with a kind of arm reaching out from the siren towards this figure's ear, ending with a starburst that would seem to represent the impact of the siren's vibrations on the ear.

I commented on the powerful emotions he had represented in the drawing—they could make hearts thump and some people were even deafened by them. I spoke also of the excitement he could perhaps feel inside himself now that he was growing into a young man; maybe he could feel his heart thumping too with all these emotions.

On the other side of the sheet of paper, he drew an enormous circular-shaped siren. He said that it looked so big because now we were seeing it close up. To the left of the siren he drew the captain warming up the turbine that triggered the siren. He blamed the captain in no uncertain terms for heating up the turbine too much, hence the siren making such a loud noise with all the disastrous consequences that then ensued.

Looking at the circular-shaped siren, I associated to a breast, and I was struck by the contrast between the ice-cold lower part and the over-heated upper part. I linked this to the therapy, reminding Alan that there was just one week left before we broke up for the long summer

Figure 8.

vacation; I added that he perhaps had the feeling that I was about to let him fall into ice-cold water (the sea/mother) if the bridge between us collapsed under the impact of over-powerful vibration-emotions.

I thought also of what his mother had told me—she had breast-fed Alan for just three days, then had stopped doing so, much against her own inclinations, on the instructions of her mother-in-law. I said to Alan that the round siren might represent a mummy's breast full of milk and that he had indeed sucked mummy's breast, but only for three days—perhaps he had the feeling that he had been shifted from a warm mummy/breast to an ice-cold mummy who was sad because she had stopped feeding her baby. I added that he was perhaps wondering whether I was about to stop giving him the good breast/food-for-thought that the sessions meant for him and drop him into the ice-cold waters of a sea/mother if ever the bridge between us started to collapse.

Conclusion

Whether we are referring to childhood autism *stricto sensu* or to the autistic enclaves described by Tustin in other pathological syndromes, the psychoanalytic exploration of this pathology leads me to suggest that there is an initial level at which psychic bisexuality becomes integrated, that of the container. Any defect in integration at this level leads to a pathology of otherness, given that one of the essential functions of the container is to enable the construction of a psychic envelope that can differentiate between the inside and the outside of the mind.

The second level of integration of bisexuality is that of part-object relations, necessary for bringing stability to the internal world. There are two kinds of link that support stabilization, the first of which I call the *nipple-link*. Corresponding to what Meltzer (1994, p. 261ff.) calls "intimacy", the nipple-link is proximal in nature and creates a relationship between the self and the nourishing maternal object. I call the second type—distal this time—the *penis-link*. I feel this term to be particularly appropriate since it echoes the relationship between the paternal part-objet and the maternal genitals in an early version of the primal scene. It creates a relationship between self and object that bridges the gap holding them apart, with their differences and their disparities. The differentiation between nipple-link and penis-link enables a complex internal world to be established in a stable fashion. In children who emerge from autism thanks to analysis, I have observed that these two kinds of link are invariably confused; to dispel this confusion requires a great deal of intensive interpretation.

The third level is that of whole-object relations. Integration of bisexuality at this level is the process that leads to the establishment of a clear-cut sexual identity. From the point of view of the mind, we become a man or a woman through identification with the same-sex parent. This should not, however, be looked on as an inflexible identification that excludes any possibility of identifying with the parent of the opposite sex. On the contrary, the very stability of our sex-based identity depends on attaining some degree of equilibrium between both kinds of identification.

CHAPTER FIVE

Comment on "Splitting of psychic bisexuality in autistic children"

Suzanne Maiello

Didier Houzel's paper takes the reader not only to the traumatic origins of autistic states, but his thoughts represent a precious contribution to the exploration of primitive mental states.

Before presenting a few comments on the paper itself, I would like to join into paying tribute to the fertility of Frances Tustin's thinking. Her legacy contains not only her ideas, but also the courage and constancy that are necessary when we embark on working with children who have withdrawn not to an "elsewhere", but into "nowhere", after their experience of a catastrophic laceration of the original container. They have disappeared into a "no-place" and a "no-time", which Houzel describes as the unconscious fantasy of an "unbridgeable discontinuity between self and object". This formulation leads to his notion of "pathology of otherness", in which self and other seem to have fallen into the same nothingness under the threat of differentiation.

The clinical material presented in the paper offers the reader the opportunity to appreciate, over the ten years of therapeutic dedication, the author's fine balance between sensitive clinical intuition and precise and creative thinking and represents a living example of what Houzel describes as *psychic bisexuality of the container.*

I would like first of all to make a brief theoretical comment on this concept. Houzel claims the existence of a level of differentiation and integration of masculine and feminine aspects, which would precede the primary split, through which the first experiences of the *other* become possible at the part object level. The author refers to a more archaic level, in which "the masculine and feminine elements are not *yet* in a relationship of penetration or respectively receptiveness, but mutually integrate each other in a tightly woven texture, in which the masculine elements reinforce the feminine container". This image evokes the very essence of the alpha-function, which contains and creates psychic links between alpha-elements, i.e., between the elements of thinkable matter.

We might wonder how it is possible that there should be an experience of "wovenness" in a mental state in which there is not yet a distinction between the interlacing threads. Bion might reply that the weaving has already occurred. The preconception of the woven container could find its first realization at the very moment it receives an embryonic thought. The first proto-mental experiences of the child seem to occur in the containment of the womb. The object of these primary experiences might well be the quality of the texture of the maternal psycho-physical container, as perceived, at the sensuous level, mainly through tactile and auditory perceptions. After birth, the psychic exploration of its qualities will be enriched by the sensations aroused by the encounter of the mouth with the breast–nipple–milk, and the visual encounter.

The clinicians who work with autistic patients seem to share the need, as Houzel puts it, to imagine a proto-mental way of functioning, which might be even more archaic than paranoid–schizoid mental states. Our endeavour is to try to mentalize and find the means to express as best we can the psycho-physical preverbal levels of experience, on whose base the primary split will unfold. In autistic states, this is the transition that is experienced as a premature and catastrophic laceration of the texture of the container and as an annihilating expulsion of the contained.

The author stresses the importance of differentiating the two primordial levels of psychic bisexuality, i.e., the level of the containing object and that of the part object. The transition from one to the other, like the transition from the part object to the whole object level, is seen as a "logical rather than a chronological precedence". Houzel suggests that in primary psychic functioning there is an oscillation between the two levels, which are seen primarily as *positions* in the Kleinian and Bionian sense, rather than as *phases*. This approach evokes Grotstein's notion of *double track* (1980), which suggests that in primitive experience, there is an alternation of mental states, one being dominated by a fantasy of primary union, and the other conveying fleeting moments of awareness of separateness.

However, Houzel's text also points to a developmental dimension in the growth of psychic functioning along the axis of time, when he states that "there can be no encounter, unless there has been a first encounter". This notion opens the space for debate on the dialectic between the temporal dimension of psychic development and the qualitative transformations of the processes and structures of mental functioning.

The second theoretical comment concerns the autistic child's experience of "unbridgeable discontinuity", which isolates him from the world of relationships among living human beings. Houzel describes the three dimensions of the *gap* existing between self and other. In the *spatial* dimension, he places the intolerable discontinuity between mouth–tongue and breast–nipple, which results from the experience of irreparability of the laceration of the container's texture. The *dynamic* level of the experience of the gap is provoked by the breach of continuity of the relationship, which, as I suggest, induces the "liquid" baby, who has no stable psychic shape of his own yet, to reach some form of stability by freezing up. The *temporal* dimension of the gap between self and object is expressed by the intolerability of any discontinuity, any temporal shift or delay in the relationship, because every postponement is experienced as a repetition of an incurable breach.

Elsewhere, I have thought about the absence of the dimension of time in autistic states, and especially about the lack of rhythmicity in the relation of these children with the world (Maiello, 2001). Rhythm has an instrinsic temporal dimension and can be described as a regular alternation of presence and absence. Tustin underlined the lack of an internal existential "rhythm of safety" in these children. I suggest that this internal rhythm can develop only when the experience of the combination of presence and absence of the primary containing object has reached a sufficient degree of stability. In other terms, the regularity of a rhythm must be sufficiently reliable for irregularities to be tolerable, and for the individual to be able not only to bear with variations of rhythm, but to discover the pleasure and creativity of improvization. The first non-catastrophic experiences of oneself as a separate living being can grow only on the secure base of a reliable continuity. I suggest that both continuity and discontinuity of rhythmical experience have specific functions for psychic development. If we connect this idea with the model proposed by Houzel, the rhythmicity of experience could be seen as one of the aspects of bisexuality, i.e., of the bi-polarity of the psychic container.

We have seen that, in autistic states, every discontinuity provokes the panic of endless falling. Annihilation anxieties result in a suspension of the exploration and proto-awareness of the texture of the primary container. The ultimate consequence of this withdrawal is the collapse of all dimensions of experience, spatial, temporal, and dynamic.

In normal development, rhythm finds its first postnatal expression in the baby's sucking at the breast, but I suggest that this experience has prenatal precursors in the unborn child's auditory and probably vibratory perceptions of the mother's voice and the rhythmic sounds of her heartbeat and breathing. The rhythmic aspects of the prenatal environment could represent the most archaic part, a sort of *basso continuo*, of the sound-object (Maiello, 1993). With this term, I describe an internal proto-object of prenatal origin, which results from the unborn child's auditory experiences in the womb.

The clinical material presented in the paper is marvellously rich in vocal, auditory, and rhythmic elements. What touched me deeply in Alan's sessions is the child's capacity to use sound and rhythmic elements not to isolate himself in sound stereotypes, as autistic children often do, but in order to communicate, in intensely evocative ways, both his catastrophic experience of the laceration of the primary union, and his efforts towards psychic reparation.

My comments on the clinical material represent an attempt to integrate the two interpretative vertices, i.e., Houzel's concept of the *bisexuality of the psychic container*, and my notion of the *polarity of continuity/discontinuity* in connection with the rhythmic aspects of the sound-object.

The first comment concerns the patient's image of the *ears*, which he assimilated to little *bells*. Alan had wondered whether there was anything he could do to prepare himself to be born, i.e., to get ready for a less catastrophic separation. The child saw himself as the *content* still contained in the maternal container, but when he said that he wanted to "prepare" himself, he showed that he knew about the existence of a temporal dimension, and of the approaching moment of leaving his autistic state.

A few sessions later, Alan changed vertex and put himself in the less dangerous position of the mouth–*container* when he spat out the water. He also threw bullets out of the room, far away, and thought that he had killed somebody, rather than being born/dying himself. However, he showed that the spatial dimension of experience was acknowledged as well.

The first signs of the child's coming out of his autistic isolation coincide with the access to the paranoid–schizoid position and hence the possibility to use projective identification in order to defend himself from primitive annihilation anxieties.

At the *oral level*, Alan enacted an expulsion, a violent separation by spitting. At the *vocal/auditory* level, he told the story of his baby sister's ears, which were like bells, and needed to be cleaned. What did the child mean by "cleaning"? He certainly wanted to expel and eliminate the therapist's voice, which had announced the end of the session. But could he also have begun to consider the possibility of cleaning out, i.e., letting go, of the autistic plug in his ears, which often makes autistic children seem deaf?

When, on the contrary, the autistic part of the personality does the "cleaning", we could say, by extending the metaphor of the bell, that the child tries to eliminate not only the unpleasant vocal content, but also, in a more radical mode, the clapper, with the result that the bell becomes mute, deaf, and useless. In other terms, the very sensitivity of the autistic child's "hearing" capacity risks being "cleaned out", not only at the sensuous, but at the psychic level. In this state, no event can be transformed into an experience, i.e., into a mentalized object.

Alan's material, on the contrary, shows that the child began to have moments of a fleeting awareness of the separability of container and contained, even though this was inevitably accompanied by persecutory anxieties. He threw out the voice that announced the separation, but his ears seemed to have maintained their potential receptivity and remained open to the return of the voice, which he was to lose at the end of the session.

The fact that the ear/bell was attributed to his baby sister may also say something about the mental level at which Alan's communication was generated. It can certainly be seen as evidence for his nascent capacity to use projective identification in order to get rid of an intolerable experience. But it is also possible that a more primitive mental level was mobilized in the child, which Houzel explored in a recent paper (2001). The author describes a primitive form of pre-oedipal rivalry towards what he called the "nest of babies". I suggest that, in the case of a premature traumatic experience of laceration of the container, its fragments themselves could be experienced as the rivals who try to expel him, the primary content, from the container and conquer his refuge for themselves.

In his comment on the session with the organ-player, which comes shortly after the session with the little bells, Houzel notes that "Alan had a very musical ear". In fact, we witness the process of the child's emotional unfreezing in the form of his vocal and rhythmic experiences.

The child produced a drawing with organ-pipes, which resembled the scheme of the session days, with which the therapist had made a graphic representation of the alternation of the presence and absence of the therapy. The child had transformed the "days" into musical notes. He sang and distinguished the high tones from low ones, as they were produced "by the air that passes through the pipes". There had been a further development in Alan's explicit perception of an internal space that had been implicit already in the image of the bell. Not only had the pipes a tridimensional volume, but air was moving through them. There was a container, both solid and vibrant, stable and receptive, and there was an alive and moving content. Both elements, the organ-pipe and the air, were necessary for a sound to be produced. A part of the child knew that a co-operative encounter had to occur between the pipe and the air, like between ear and voice, bell and clapper, mouth and nipple, in order to produce an encounter and a rhythm of reciprocity.

The therapist recognized the melodious line of Alan's singing and "playing". It was a fugue by Bach. A fugue is a composition in which the theme is reintroduced, deferred in time. The deferment in itself introduces the principle of alternation of presence and absence, of sequentiality instead of temporal coincidence, but the number of measures between the first presentation of the theme and its reintroductions is stable, so that the deferment occurs at a constant and reliable rhythm.

In Alan's experience, the rythmical constancy of the therapist's psychic container seemed to have allowed the child to become aware of differentiations that in the past had entailed catastrophic lacerations, and to create connections, which gradually reinforced the texture of the container and brought about the possibility to tolerate some feeling of separateness.

The German language offers an unexpected encounter point between the vertex of the bisexuality of the psychic container and the vertex of the different aspects of the sound-object, in the terms it uses to designate the tonalities of the Western tonal system. In German, the major and the minor key are called *Dur* and *Moll*, hard and soft, and evoke respectively the firmness and the flexibility of the musical container–contained.

Three years later, the theme of the little bell was taken up once more by the child, but at a more integrated level of mental functioning. Alan talked about some sessions that had to be cancelled. Once the absence can be named, it is no longer a bottomless abyss. This time, the little ear/bells had become church bells. They were silent before Easter, but started tolling again on Easter day, "because Jesus had resurrected".

The sound of a tolling bell is intermittent by nature, but presence and absence alternate at regular intervals. It is like the beating of a heart. Alan still associated the silent bells with death, but at a new level of experience, if compared to the ear/bells that needed to be cleaned of whatever threatening content. Now, Alan knew that after the silence, the bells would toll again. He trusted their approaching movement in *space* (from Rome to Caen), and in *time* (resurrection after death). The experience of the continuity of the rhythm of his therapy seemed by now to allow him to begin to tolerate its discontinuities.

In fact, the sound of the bell that goes away but comes back, and whose structure of container–contained remains intact in its duality, gives evidence of the onset of introjective processes in the child.

His sound-object has become more reliable. By integrating the idea of the rhythmical bipolarity of the sound-object with Houzel's model of psychic bisexuality, I suggest that Alan had been born, or reborn, thanks to the reparative experience of a more solid interweaving of the two basic qualities of the psychic container, i.e., receptive flexibility and structuring firmness.

The more recent sessions are a moving testimony to the patient's efforts to save his fragile internal objects from breaking down again under the pressure of the emotional turbulence of puberty. Once more, the struggle is expressed at the musical and auditory level. The very existence of the sound-object in both its musical and rhythmic aspect seems to be threatened.

The military airs, which are tuned by definition to the rhythm of marching feet, were associated with the grandfather, Alan's *Bon Papa,* and seemed a more active masculine–paternal re-edition of the ringing bells of his childhood. If ringing bells have a rocking and calming effect, military airs evoke an idea of strength and underline the act of walking. The element which the two musical expressions have in common is their rhythmic reliability.

With the powerful sound of the penetrating oedipal father–helicon on the one hand, and on the other the burps into the uncle's ears, which seem to express phantasies of oral sexual promiscuity, Alan continued to produce material of auditory and vocal character, which gives evidence of the psychic complexity and ambivalence of his preadolescent mental state.

The pubertal boy was both attracted and frightened by the powerful paternal *presence*, but the re-emergence of the *absence* of the paternal aspect of the primary container resuscitated the primitive self's despair and anxiety of endless falling. The absence of the lifeguards on the beach seemed to announce the panic that was to be provoked, one year later, by the unbearable whining of the siren, which emitted its terrifying sound at fixed times. However, its regularity had lost any rhythmic quality.

Alan was precipitated once more into the abyss of his primitive annihilation anxieties. The bridge, which should have connected the two shores, collapsed. This is the breakdown which leads to what Houzel describes as the "unbridgeable discontinuity between self and object", which characterizes autistic states. The roughly sketched human beings on his drawing were precipitated into the ice-cold water of the sea/mother amidst the unbearable sounds of the siren. The image evokes the new-born baby Alan who had lost the access to the breast across the bridging nipple. He may well have felt as if falling from his depressed mother's arms and mind when he lost the breast three days after birth. But Alan's traumatic experience was even more complex, and he was capable of representing it with surprising and moving precision. Not only was the volume of the sound of the siren unbearable for his ears, but so were the vibrations that it emanated. Alan explained that the emissions of the siren reached both the ears and "heart in the chest" of the precipitated people. One of them was deafened by the impact of vibrations, and the hearts of others were exposed to emotions too violent to bear.

Alan seemed to describe the effect of the cries of a baby, which echo in his ears and head and accelerate his breathing and heartbeat as an effect of both effort and panic. Everything cries, everything vibrates, the sounds and rhythms are disorganized and fragmented and collapse under the violence of annihilation anxieties. Tustin writes about her "heartbroken" autistic patients by saying that the breach goes far beyond its usual metaphoric meaning.

> The feeling of brokenness goes into the very fabric of their being . . . Since the sucking rhythm had become associated with the beating of the heart, it was the "teat–tongue–heart" that was felt to be broken. . . . For these patients, bodily awareness of their separateness had been experienced as an interruption to the pulsing rhythm of their "going-on-being". [Tustin, 1990, p. 156]

Tustin's formulation brings the two vertices together, i.e., the experience of a premature laceration of the texture of the container, and the loss of the basic sense of existential rhythmicity.

At the time, Alan had defended himself against his catastrophic experience as best he could. But now he had become able to tell his therapist not only about the trauma of the breakdown of the unconscious fantasy of the existence of a bridge towards the world, but also to represent the primitive autistic defences with which he had tried to contrast his overwhelming annihilation anxieties.

If "bad sounds" are too loud, autistic withdrawal can bring about both muteness and psychic deafness, and if the violence of emotions causes unbearable vibrations, they can both be frozen up in a petrified heart, which is no longer accessible. This is the state which Houzel describes as "pathology of otherness". One of its consequences is the death or a form of hibernation of the sound-object in both its vocal–auditory and rhythmic articulations.

Can we think of a more precise way of describing the tragedy of autistic retreat? Alan has been able to do so thanks to the quality of his therapist's mental containment, which combined maternal receptivity and paternal firmness.

CHAPTER SIX

Conversation with Geneviève Haag

Introduced by Hélène and Alexandre Dubinsky

Hélène and Alexandre Dubinsky began by referring to the profound influence which the work of Geneviève Haag has exerted on the psychoanalytic treatment of autistic children, on infant observation, and, more generally, on the understanding of primitive anxieties in children and adults who are not on the autistic spectrum. To begin the discussion, they asked her to speak on three questions: on the containing function, with special reference to excitability in children with autism; on the meaning of children passing a ball from one hand to the other (as illustrated in Anne Alvarez' presentation); and on the issue of the gradual development of the mind, and those factors which make for its gradual nature.

Geneviève Haag

I will start with the question of why I believe that development is gradual—and this is an opinion, I think, that many of us share. Every living being unfolds like a plant, like a tree. I do not believe that everything is present or given at the beginning of life, except perhaps as potential. On the other hand, our efforts to analyse the course of development, starting from naturalistic or clinically-based observation, can suggest many hypotheses.

My own experiences with children and adolescents with autism have led me to recognize that excitability is an important feature, and that the containment of arousal and of instinct can easily break down. This leads us to the issue of introjection in children with autism, which Anne Alvarez highlighted in her presentation. I would like to take further a question that has already been much discussed, namely the question of those earliest introjections that seem particularly related to the containing function. Freud addressed this in relation to the protective shield; many French colleagues, along with Esther Bick and Anzieu, speak of the skin; Bion refers to "container–contained". What aroused my own curiosity was the realization that this containing function was related to the development of the body ego in ways we continue to study. All children with autism who begin to establish or re-establish relationships show us how fundamental sensory experiences lead to the feeling of being contained, of being enveloped by something "all around" one, like a kind of hoop that permits bodily arousal to be stabilized. Often this means the disappearance or at least the substantial reduction of stereotypic behaviours, which, as we know, serve the function of allowing children with autism to cope with existing in space: without these rhythmical repetitions they feel that they are falling, unless they can discover or re-discover the self-containing function that arises from the earliest introjection of the other's containing function. All these children seem to tell the same story: it isn't the first thing they show us, but one of the first—as I have written, we discover many things backwards. The question of a bodily axis, and the way the two halves of the body come to be attached to each other by means of identificatory processes entering into the construction of the body ego, then became progressively clearer (Haag, 1985). After that, I was struck by recurring material of autistic children who were coming back into contact, and which implied that it was important to take account of hearing as well as of the tactile experiences. I had been thinking about Suzanne Maiello's work on the prenatal sound object, and her remarkable clinical observations point up the sudden emergence of rhythmical structures. Unlike autistic stereotypies, they occur in the context of relationships and are accompanied by phenomena of a musical order. After this, or, rather, following on from this, children show a new daring in moving through space. This implies that sound is an integral part of the tactile envelope that, as the children's material showed, was in the process of developing sphericization in the course of emotional exchanges mediated by eye-to-eye interpenetrating contact. Such developments are possible only if the child feels we are responding to something he conveys to us. Often we experience the child's communications on a bodily level that precedes projection; at best, this may involve some emotion, but largely it is a matter of muscular tone, of hallucinosis, of feeling that we are falling, of many such things that the child needs us to understand. These first instances of understanding on our part seem to lead the child to perceive rhythms that grow out of the relationship and that can become mentalized. Otherwise children have to survive by means of rhythms that are purely kinaesthetic, auditory, or proprioceptive, and which they keep going by spinning in circles.

It took several years to gather these data, to find the bodily dimension to those first introjections that caused Freud to speak of a body ego, though I still do not fully understand his reference to the ego as a surface phenomenon. I believe that it is only through these findings of the past two or three decades that we are beginning to deepen our understanding of the body ego that, at the same time, is already the self. Children show us that it is within the space of this "hoop" that comes into being around them that they can begin to dramatize.

I would like to give a brief clinical vignette from a paper written a long time ago. The child concerned had come to treatment in a state of appalling rigidity. Once the first introjection I have been speaking of was formed or rediscovered, he was able to show me that his former posture—which looked as though he were petrified, almost crucified—meant being stuck to a wall and with his fingers clutching on to a moulding. The emotionally significant eye-contact between us while he was showing me this was accompanied by a sweeping movement of his arms that brought both thumbs up to his mouth: the resurgence of oral auto-erotism almost always accompanies the constitution or reconstitution of the psychic envelope. Until now he was perched on a tiny ledge, as though he were a mountaineer clinging to the rock face. Just after showing me in this way that a feeling of being emotionally met came together with his two thumbs in his mouth, and that a platform or floor was beginning to exist, he went to sit cross-legged on a wide piece of furniture. He asked me for Fisher-Price beads, which he slotted together in a circle around himself, then gestured to me to pass him toy figures for a piece of dramatic play. This seems to me a very speaking image for the way in which the introjection of the containing function, as soon as it takes place, can underpin the much more elaborated symbolic level of dramatization.

The mystery is why children with autism remain susceptible to spilling over emotionally, even after a long time in treatment. The degree of this tendency brings to mind Freud's reference to biological bedrock. Perhaps they are pre-disposed to particularly rich sensory experience, and have lived through circumstances that made the containing function very difficult to establish. Now, the bodily axis and the process by which the two sides of the body are attached to each other are established (and demonstrated during therapy) within the framework of the basic containing function. This is what I have called "the mother and baby in two halves of the body" (Haag, 1985). What, then, is taking place when the baby takes objects we offer him, or when he passes them back and forth between his two hands? Within his own body, I think, he is playing out the emotional exchanges with the other in all their rhythmicity. Playing with a ball or with rings that can be passed from one hand to the other is a very important game of basic introjection. It precedes and underpins the baby's ability to move through the space that separates two people in order to give the other person an object and to take it back: a bridge consisting of exchanges between two people which it is necessary for him to master. This happens at the end of the first year of life, the point at which small children hand us things. (It is important for us not to keep hold of these things for too long: there remains a slight danger that primitive anxieties could make the child feel that the objects were being torn away.) So, in my view, the game described by Anne Alvarez indicates incorporation and introjection; not incorporation in the pathological sense of the word, but in the sense of incorporation into the body ego that goes before or accompanies an introjection.

This whole question of primary introjections is very closely linked with the development of the containing function and of bodily links. It is also important that this is a first link: the link of eye contact is perceived as an interpenetration, and is incarnated in the joints of the body (Haag, 1991). People with autism are not subject to the splitting of schizophrenics: this has already been highlighted by a number of authors, including Meltzer. Often, "splitting" is a term reserved for schizophrenia. The bodies of people with autism are divided up according to the natural location of the joints, not into pieces that are shredded as though by a sadistic schizophrenic explosion. Various clinicians have remarked on this: the process is something that can take place—or be reversed—more easily than psychotic splits, which deteriorate to a much more profound degree. Bion's bizarre objects are conglomerates formed from the torn away fragments that have recombined. I do not believe that bizarre objects occur in autism.

[A question from the floor concerning the difference with respect to splitting between autism and schizophrenia]

First of all, I want to refer to Meltzer's work on the dismantling of the perceptual apparatus accompanied by a relaxation of attention, and leading the child with autism to cling to a light or a sound. Meltzer showed that it was a matter of the relaxation of attention, not of a sadistic attack on perceptual processes. Children with autism can feel that they have no skin, or that they have been cut in two: it is in the context of this experience of being cut in two that the question of the construction of the body image takes on the importance it has. Being cut in two, then, means not feeling integrated; one could speak of the contrast between this kind of unintegration and the disintegration that implies an explosion. Connections within the body ego are formed through the incorporation or introjection of links. For example, in adhesive identification with the body of the actual mother, the hand belonging to the "mother" side of the child's body may envelop or be enveloped by the child's other hand. The kind of game that ensues is characteristic of normal babies between three and nine months, and seems to contribute to the experience of the vertical body axis and of a unified body ego. A little girl with autism showed me for four months that she did not feel properly "stuck together" down the centre of her body. Since at the time I had no conception of these processes, I did not understand her when she showed me that she had to squeeze herself because she did not feel properly joined at the midline like the little toy dolls' house which could open and shut on its midline hinges. I could not conceive of the existence of such a problem. But she kept on showing me that things were stuck together, not stuck, joined, squeezed, until finally I asked her, "Are you worried about not being properly stuck together down the middle?" And immediately she stopped the repetitive play sequences that had occurred in every session for the past three or four months. In other words, she had been unable fully to construct this central bodily join: her play was an elaborative recapitulation of something that had partly come up between us. This girl had already re-fashioned her envelope by means of eye contact, looking into my eyes deeply and with concentration while she held a little piece of blue card. Then she indicated that she felt enveloped, and immediately attempted to unite the two sides of her body. This, as she showed me, was what was so difficult, so that for a long time she continued to cling to the reflections of light in the window-pane. This kind of process can be reversed many times. The complicating factor is that a certain number of adolescent or adult schizophrenics have problems in the area of the body image involving the experience of being cut in two. I think that this is a more autistic aspect of schizophrenia. For example, Gisela Pankow and Marion Milner describe how such patients suffer through feeling cut in two and being forced or obliged to establish a symbiosis between half of their body and the analyst's body. Children with autism show us this when they take our hand to do something that they cannot do for themselves. At that point, they have the need to "stick" half of their body concretely on to the therapist's body. If we can continue an emotional interchange, continue to understand the process of sticking on to us while it is happening and the anxieties that underlie it, then bit by bit they can reconstruct their bodily axis and regain possession of both halves of their body. Normal babies go through this process of separating half of their body from that of their mother between the ages of three and nine months, in the context of auto-erotism. When normal babies do not feel well, their limbs do not cross over, they lie flat and tense in their cradles or with their backs against the floor. Professionals with whom I do preventive work agree that we need to be worried about these isolated babies who spread themselves flat on the floor and don't cross their hands or feet. We learn from infant observation that games involving the crossing over of hands, the dramatization of relationship that hands can enact around the middle of the body, tend to appear precisely after intense emotional contact. This is a natural median axis for division and joining because it involves developmental achievements in relation to the body image, while schizophrenics will have a body image that involves shredding bits that are torn away, that bleed; bits that are cut off. Oral erotism linked to biting is much more in the ascendant, and so are issues of symbiosis linked to oral and anal sadism.

[Question from the floor: If this is the erotic component of schizophrenic splitting, which erotic component is involved in the autistic child's "failure to cross over"?]

This "failure to cross over" stems from the freezing of the oral instincts. Many have noted this freezing in autism, such that instinctual development hardly gets under way. Thus we observe the evasion of eye contact, the "amputation" of the oral erogenous zone, the resort to the muscles and to skin sensations in the service of clinging: all manifestations of the absence of oral instinctual vitality—or rather of its minimal development, as I don't believe that its total absence is compatible with survival. But it is present to a truly minimal degree, and when autistic children begin to thaw out, they are flooded by oral instinctual manifestations, as is the case with any instinctual awakening. This aspect of instinctual thawing can be very difficult: we witness explosions that Frances Tustin described as "volcanic"; oral phenomena that are too strong; excessively strong projective identification that makes for an unavoidable period of post-autistic psychosis. This can take various forms: sometimes, though rarely, it can be of a schizophrenic type, though without the manifestations of "paradoxicalité". On the other hand, a manic psychosis can easily be triggered.

I have attempted to understand more about the amputation of bodily zones in autism, as I asked myself what brought about these mouths that I had called "muzzles", these mouths which seemed to have been amputated. In the most severe cases of autism, we can observe mouths without any muscular tone, an absence of sucking or, sometimes, the sucking of deep-lying parts of the tongue; something that goes on between the jaws; clicking perhaps; but the surrounds of the mouth seem to have disappeared. As Winnicott (1963) said, even in normal early development, the mother's absence can be experienced as the loss of the baby's zone of oral contact: the mouth can be lost along with the mother. This loss of the oral erogenous zone does not just follow from the mother's physical absence: it can also follow from the mother's emotional absence or from problems in establishing a link in feeling. I am not talking about aetiology. Something is not taking place in this early emotional interplay, in the sensuous interchanges that are already emotional, as Frances Tustin has described. The important thing is that the baby should feel that something is returned to him once eye contact is established. It is as though the baby experienced this in spatial terms: as though something took place behind the mother's eyes, so that, if nothing is returned, this means there is no foundation, no backing, to her head: the baby's communication gets lost, it falls out of her head on the other side. Many children with autism have shown me that they felt they fell down if the therapist's eyes could be travelled through without anything being returned to them. In some cases, one suspects that the erogenous zone is in a state of tension with regard to a motor image, as though it seemed to travel towards the mother's head and then fall out the other side—a powerful thought. The negative hallucination of some of the autistic child's amputated body parts, then, might not be due to an oral tearing away, but to something like a primal bodily–psychic interchange that I have called "relational rhythm" and that isn't working properly. Some of you may share my experience of children with autism who are starting to make contact: we lean towards them for a conversation that they are beginning to tolerate, an exchange of glances that they are beginning to accept, and we see a child who had never before sucked his thumb and who now begins to do so, not because we have offered him a bottle in the course of "corrective regression", but simply because the to-and-fro of glances has got under way. This is what led me to suggest that the thumb does not just represent the nipple in the mouth, but all the emotional exchanges mediated by eye contact that accompany what Meltzer (1986) called the double interpenetration (of eye–eye and nipple–mouth), which is so important for the first introjections.

[Question from the floor: Could you say more about the two halves of the baby—the baby-half and the mother-half—that are linked by the central bodily axis?]

I base this idea on evidence from three sources: the direct observation of infants, the treatment of children with autism, and the analysis of adults. Neurotic or borderline adults on the couch can undergo processes of depersonalization in which they tell us about these bodily experiences. There can be a "big side" and a "little side", or else, as Grotstein described in relation to the "background object", there can be the experience of losing the back of the body. There are the phenomena that I have already described in relation to babies. Then there is the behaviour of children with autism who are beginning to make contact, and who lean half of their body, usually the dominant half, on the body of the therapist as soon as some measure of the containing function has been established. This is a long process of separation which comes about—and shows itself—through emotional sharing mediated by eye contact; through auto-erotic consolidation in the interlacing of the hands; above all, in the way that one hand relates to the other. Perhaps the most convincing finding from infant observation is one I have mentioned several times, when babies in the second half of the first year of life are in the process of consolidating these developments but still seem to feel that their dominant side is confused with the mother's body–mind, probably adhesively. This occurs when they cannot anticipate when the mother will move away. When they can anticipate this, we can see them putting their auto-erotic backup in place: they suck their thumb, join their two hands, begin to manipulate objects with crossing-over at the midline. But if the mother moves away suddenly, if the telephone rings, for example, she jumps up from her chair and we can see the dominant side of the baby leave with her, as though drawn by a magnet, while with the other hand the baby catches hold of its dominant arm and tries to pull it back. We could call this an adhesive identification of the dominant side of the baby during the process of introjection of bodily links. This is what I have called intra-corporeal identifications, and this holds true in the first year of life. During the second year, the symbolization is different: the right side of the body tends to be assimilated to the father, and the left side to the mother, while, on the deeper level, the paternal elements are located in the bodily axis. Several presentations in the course of this conference have illustrated the fact that relational interpenetration and issues to do with the background form part of the register of paternal elements. Children with autism illustrate this beautifully by showing how the penetrating aspect of the gaze links to characteristics of the play material—interlocking cubes, for example, or putting the pencils in a beaker ; then they will show you that pencils represent the bodily axis: they put them to face their axis, looking you full in the eye—laughing as if showing you this gives them pleasure—and those who are beginning to speak a bit will say, "Daddy". Normal children in the second year of life show us how they locate these bisexual elements in objects and in architecture. I always think of a little girl of eighteen months who arrived for her session with her father, brandishing the central stalk of a toy on to which rings could be threaded. She jumped up, showed me the stalk, and said, "Daddy". In the room, she told me about each piece of furniture whether it was "Daddy" or "Mummy". "Daddy" was door-handles, hinges, and corners, the angles of furniture; "Mummy" was round cushions, everything soft. Truly, bisexual elements are distributed within the body and in projections on to objects: and there too, it is not purely a matter of bodily experience, but of bodily–mental experience. From the beginning, identifications are important: the body is not a given. It has to be progressively constructed in parallel with the mind. We may recall Freud's statement that the ego is first and foremost a body ego; but I think that we have only begun to understand the detail since people have begun to treat autistic children.

[Question from the floor, concerning a sixteen-year-old girl who is not autistic, though she speaks little, but whose body is lifeless and whose glance is empty. Her dreams contain instances of mutilated bodies.]

This is a more complex problem: the dream material implies an extremely sadistic attack on the body, and that this comes back at this girl in the form of an inhibition, or perhaps an annihilation rather than an inhibition. You describe an absence of muscular tone, something like a complete liquefaction of tone. This is probably not an autistic process. It sounds more as though there were a dissociation between what can emerge in the patient's dreams and a type of depression, which may follow extreme attacks on internal objects. This can be no more than hypothetical, since I do not know the context of the material. In autistic conditions, experiences of liquefaction or of a related lack of muscular tone seem to be compensated for, more or less in reflex fashion, by bodily rigidity. For this adolescent, it seems to be an internal matter and more complex, probably a type of depression following on from the terrible attacks that she describes in her dreams and which may re-awaken a primary depression. By this I mean a depression experienced in bodily terms as falling and liquefying.

[Question from the floor: The problem in autism concerning oral instinctual development, of which Tustin's "amputation of the mouth" is an example, makes us wonder what takes place beforehand, in terms of skin and second skin. Bick refers to muscular second skin; McDougall to the muscular ego. Rather than thinking in terms of attachment or ethology, would it be useful to posit a libidinal stage involving the musculature, before the oral stage, which might be the fixation point for those reaction formations that children with autism make use of in their encounters with us?]

I believe that kinaesthetic phenomena form part of the first prenatal structures, of what we might imagine as constituting an embryonic form of awareness of existing, a prenatal embryonic self. There is the skin, there are kinaesthetic experiences. Meltzer refers to the "song and dance level", that is, those experiences of muscular rhythmicity which are already present in prenatal activity. The trauma of birth interrupts this for a time: the inner ear and the sense of balance are disrupted, and so is kinaesthetic experience. The feeling of falling, the action of gravity, what Bullinger calls gravitational flux, suddenly immobilize something that used to be mobile and introduce the need for rigidity. Kinaesthetic pleasure no doubt comes together with the sound envelope and with what is experienced on the level of the skin; finally, we have pressure on the skin of the back. All children with autism show us that support for the back comes first, and that eye contact follows. Kinaesthesia is part of very early development, but comes into its own once the containing function has been introjected. Beginning in the second month, babies' movements are far more relaxed, and no longer depend so greatly on the tonic reflex of the neck. I am talking like a physiologist, but this is necessary: this is a level that remains embedded in us as a model of self-support. Once the envelope has been formed, babies' pleasure in being naked becomes obvious, whereas previously, the trauma of birth makes us feel we have lost our skin. The skin must be refashioned, and this can only happen in the context of bodily–mental experience through the introjection of the containing function processed inside the development of oral sexuality, which, I believe, begins in prenatal life: skin and mouth are constructed at the same time. If there is no problem, muscular tone no longer needs to be used to counteract the experience of falling; it is impressive to witness. Whether these muscular phenomena constitute a true regression, I am not sure. Stiffening appears to me to be more a "pathological" defence. Besides, some kinds of prenatal shock can immobilize a pre-term foetus. Along with the danger to survival, there is a semi-reflex stiffening that, in fact, does link with theories of attachment as well as with Hermann's theories concerning clinging. Esther Bick talked about "holding on to survive": this can be muscular or sensory, and is resorted to in the face of primitive anxieties that have not been dealt with through the primal introjections.

[Question from the floor, concerning the therapist's experience of physical sensations in the course of treating autistic children]

This is something I touched on yesterday, when we were discussing what might "circulate" before projective identification, before the construction of three-dimensionality. My hypothesis arises through having experienced very distressing bodily sensations during the treatment of children with autism. I have come to think that there is some kind of transmission of experience, which is why I posit a normal two-dimensionality, where sensations, associated with some sort of emotional component, already "circulate". For example, when the child seems lost in his stereotypies, the therapist may feel herself liquefying to the extent of hardly being able to sit up, and of needing to use the arm-rests of the chair, or to sit down on the floor with her back against the wall, in order to manage. I think there is the moment, just as in projective identification, where one starts by thinking, "I'll have a temperature of 101 tonight, I'm going to have to stop the session, this is ghastly, I'm incubating something." Or one thinks, "I didn't sleep properly last night, that's all it is." One looks for personal reasons for feeling as one does. Then, if this goes on for two or three sessions, one ends up thinking that the child is conveying something of the nature of his primitive bodily anxiety, which is to do with spilling out, or falling, through the "liquefying" absence of muscular tone. I think we need to verbalize this, even to dramatize it. If we can truly convey that we are the child who feels he is spilling out, if we dramatize this by calling for help, we can see how the child abandons his stereotypical movements and turns towards us. We have to repeat the dramatization for a while for the child to be sure that we have understood. This kind of suffering makes children with autism turn to stereotypies in the search for a kinaesthetic means of survival.

[Question from the floor: Could you say more about your understanding of normal two-dimensionality?]

I think this area is related to André Green's concept of "excorporation" which affects the body, and probably also to the experience of muscular tone which is—or is not—sufficient to support oneself. Other examples might be such sensory experiences as taking pleasure in light, which sometimes can go as far as visually clinging on to a light source; or again any kind of rhythmical pleasure in light or in sound, which does not, I think, presuppose three-dimensionality. These can be observed before children in treatment, or normal babies in the course of development, have introjected the containing function. Why should pre-natal emotional experiences on the "song-and-dance" level not be communicable within the rhythms of "surface" experiences, without the need to assume that three-dimensionality has been constructed, reconstructed, or, occasionally, lost, at a very early stage? My own feeling is that three-dimensionality is present, but completely normal babies can be seen to cling on to sense impressions when they do not feel sufficiently held. This rhythmical exchange shows in the earliest graphic traces. I believe that they indicate a surface level of experience, and simultaneously, or very soon afterwards, a focus on points that represent interpenetration. We can observe rounded shapes, or spiral movements concerned with depth. For example, an autistic child who was re-enacting the process of achieving a feeling of containment provided me with a very beautiful illustration that I have already written about two or three times. He produced what I have called "returning loops" (*boucles de retour*), which imply that one has found something within the other person's head that one can bounce off, so that the feelings one has communicated do not get lost, but are returned to one. This child produced successive loops, so that they seemed to constitute an enveloping function. It is the accumulation of such rhythmical experience that eventually leads to a feeling of being enclosed, and this feeling implies fundamental rhythmical structures on a sensory–emotional level.

Another example concerns the girl I have called Paula, who made use of net curtains. She began by illustrating the importance of sound rhythms, in accordance with Suzanne Maiello's hypotheses: she indicated a loss of communication by means of sound by stretching the telephone wire to its limit and then dropping it. In contrast, when she felt that communication between us had been re-established, she repeatedly stretched out the wire and then used it to bring back the telephone. Then she wrapped herself up in half of the net curtain, took hold of the receiver, and used it to create a rhythm within the curtain that enveloped her. It was only now that she drew my colleague and me, one after the other, closer inside the curtain in order to be able to "dive" into our eyes: that rounded out the experience of being surrounded, contained. Once this process had taken place, she could push us further away inside the other half of the curtain: her skin could begin to separate from ours. This separation or division of skins, or of "shells", is mysterious and very impressive; several presentations have touched on it. Once the feeling of being enveloped has been achieved, the skin can "double up" and separate out: Anzieu has pointed this out too. That doesn't mean that the child's whole body has separated out; but the feeling of being enveloped means that the child's head can feel separate somewhere between the second and fifth month of life. Now projection can come into play. A level of experience exists in which one launches something outwards, there is to-ing and fro-ing and then there is a bridge: children with autism show us this very clearly. It's the story of the construction of space, where the gaze leaps into the other's eyes; if one is to dare this leap, one needs to be sure that there will be somewhere to land. And if one is not to fall out on the other side, this somewhere, the head of the other person, must have a backing, a foundation.

[Question from the floor: In our service, one of the earliest signs that make us think that autism might develop is a lack of muscular tone. How could we suggest to therapists and paediatric physiotherapists that they might work with these six-month-old babies who, as soon as one approaches them or pulls them into a sitting position, go floppy with arms wide apart?]

This is a problem of prevention that goes much further than autism. I think these reactions in the first months of life are not necessarily the beginning of an autistic withdrawal, but they certainly do indicate a fragility of the earliest structures. If nothing is done, various signs of psychopathology may be observed in the second year of life. Children who were rigid or limp as babies may be overly agitated and overly aggressive. Then one remembers how they used to stiffen up, and one realizes that their introjection of the containing function is very weak. I tend to advise not touching the baby's body too much, but to emphasize emotional to-and-fro with him. In a nursery, it can be enough to say, "listen to this baby, try to find a bit more time for him, for those moments of emotional 'conversation'". We see the baby's body lose its stiffness, or become more tonic, bodily "cross-overs" make their appearance, it can be quite amazing. In some cases where there is gaze avoidance and problems with listening, we might be witnessing the beginnings of an autistic syndrome; but it would be wrong to expect this, because recovery can be very quick. At a conference in Toulouse concerning violence, I described the case of a little girl between the ages of eighteen months and three years who was one of the most violent children I have come across. She wrenched objects away from other children, and was incapable of playing or of bringing two objects together: she seemed completely given over to aggression and hyperactivity. In this case, I managed, after some difficulty, to establish a connection with the mother. Meanwhile, the nursery staff did their best to attract the child to the possibility of an understanding relationship. She took a long time to accept this, but little by little, we could see that she stopped wrenching things away from other children or invading them. And indeed, children like this do invade other people's territory in a sadistic, despoiling way. One senses that they do not feel that they exist within their own space: whatever one gives them, even if it is the same thing other children have, doesn't count. The feeling of existing is attached to the other's possessions, to the other's space, and that is where these children feel they need to be. First of all, this little girl stopped invading other children's territory; then, one day, the staff told me that she was no longer aggressive except in self-defence. In other words, she now had a space of her own, and she could defend it. By the time she was two and a half or three, and about to transfer to school, her balance and confidence were restored. And, in some sense, she realized what had taken place. She gave me the kind of demonstration one sometimes comes across in normal children between eighteen months and two years, who refer to the containing function by means of architectural structures. They make use of walls, of doors, of comings and goings, they run all the way to the end of the flat and bring their hands up against the wall there as though locating a foundation; they come back and set off again. The capacity for sphincterization has developed: doors perhaps represent this best of all, but there is also the far end of the flat, which really represents the precursors of sphincterization, with the elements of a wall that can serve as a foundation, of a floor, and of coming and going. This little girl had realized what my role was: a combination of paying attention to her and of supporting those who fulfilled a maternal function for her. Standing next to a paddling-pool filled with balls, she looked straight at me, then plunged into it. Pointing her nose upwards, she ran to the end of the room and felt the solidity of the wall. She returned and plunged back into the pool; and, interestingly, another child, where we had worried about a possible autistic withdrawal, who was fragile in the same way, immediately followed her example. Both of them went through the same sequence four or five times. The last time, she stayed on the edge of the pool and pretended to fall out of it. I went up to her, and whispered, discreetly, "I remember, you used to be frightened of falling." She gave me a big smile and stopped her demonstration.

CHAPTER SEVEN

Conversation with Raymond Cahn

Introduced by François Marty (EFPP Conference, Caen, September 2001)

François Marty

Introducing Raymond Cahn is very difficult for a number of reasons. The first is that reading and re-reading his work engenders a feeling of familiarity that discourages a critical stance. It is as though we had always known what he is telling us. My understanding of this is that we all need to re-interpret his approach to adolescence, to rediscover it, to create it for ourselves (or to imagine that we are doing so). In many cases, we realize that our own supposed discoveries are only a rediscovery of suggestions he made many years previously, when he opened up approaches that could help us to think about such difficult questions as the relationship between adolescence and psychosis. This makes for the first difficulty in introducing someone whose work makes us feel that we are very close to him.

Second, those of you who know his writings will be familiar with the breadth of his culture and of his range of reference, which includes literature, mythology, and history as well as psychoanalysis.

Finally, the field opened up by Raymond Cahn's work is more complex than one might assume. His thought comprises an intellectual journey: his first area of interest was not adolescence. His intellectual development, as the reader discovers, is the result of a remarkable developmental trajectory on many levels—personal, clinical, and professional.

Raymond Cahn is a psychiatrist and psychoanalyst, and *membre titulaire* of the Paris Psychoanalytic Society, of which he was President in 1979–1980. For many years he has served on the editorial committees of the journals *Revue Française de Psychanalyse* and *Adolescence*, and you will find many of his papers there, though not only there. At one point, he was tempted to train as a paediatrician: it is worth noting that adolescence is not an area that presents itself to begin with, either in the history of psychoanalysis or in the professional history of psychoanalysts who have opened up the field. Cahn soon turned to psychiatry and psychoanalysis: he worked first with children, later with adolescents. It follows that in his clinical practice and theoretical formulations adolescence is in no way sequestered from the rest of emotional life or from related areas of study. In many ways, Raymond Cahn is close to Winnicott: in his relationship to childhood and paediatrics, and also because of his independence of mind. He is the very opposite of a member of a clique, and it is a valuable lesson for us to see that it is possible to develop intellectually, as a clinician and as a theoretician without confining oneself to a single way of approaching the complex issues we deal with.

You all know his clinical work, which largely concerns adolescence, and, more particularly, work in institutions. We owe him much for developing the notion of institutional space that not only serves as a transitional area between patient and therapist, but that also involves the psychological dynamics of the carers and of the group of resident patients. This may seem evident to us now, but it is to him that we owe the exploration of this area.

Cahn's work on the relationship between psychosis and adolescence increasingly led him to question the relationship between the subject and the outside world, and also between the subject and his own consitutional difficulties. This led him to his striking formulations concerning the process of *subjectification*. These arose out of his original view on psychosis, which led him to reverse the usual approach and to come at psychosis by considering subjectivity. Subjectification is far from being an obscure neologism: Raymond

Cahn himself, as he has explained to me, sees subjectification as the negative of objectification. This does not sum up the complexity of the question, but it may serve as a way of approaching his thinking in all the areas I have mentioned, as well as the much wider area of psychosis itself, on which he will have much to teach us in the future.

Raymond Cahn

Thank you for this introduction, which hardly leaves me the possibility of mystifying you! Instead of talking in detail about the concept of subjectification, I would like to free-associate together with you before inviting questions: interchange is a better way for things to become clear. This conference is concerned with psychosis or pre-psychosis, more perhaps in children than in adolescents. My own chief interest has been in adolescents, and I have seen things not so much in terms of psychotic and pre-psychotic problems, important though these are, as from the perspective of a derailment of the process of subjectification.

Freud and Jones saw adolescence as the final developmental stage, that of genitality. This was supposed to involve some sort of recapitulation and extension of previous developments, those of the first years of life. I feel increasingly that this quite deterministic viewpoint, according to which everything important is supposed to have occurred at the very beginning, does not do justice to our observations. Very important things can happen later on, as *après-coup*, and particularly in adolescence. Many structural constraints exist, much is predetermined; but there is also the unforeseen, modification is always possible, psychic constituents can always be re-worked. Conversely, circumstances can arise in adolescence that lead to definitive fixations and consolidations. Adolescence is a critical time of life, involving instinctual transformations concerning the discovery of genitality; problems of identity; issues concerning one's place *vis-à-vis* the other, face to face with the object. On the other hand, the role of the environment and the importance of the object are undisputed. This unstable equilibrium between inside and outside is a fundamental aspect of adolescence, that time when everything can be re-examined, when familiar constellations can be re-worked with the possibility of idiosyncratic creations. As far as the object is concerned, there is a constant oscillation between nostalgia for the old, Oedipal object, and impulses towards new objects. Equally, the sense of identity can be re-worked or enriched, and the fundamental issue can be addressed of whether and how far a conscious and pre-conscious space can develop that can be used to maximum effect. It is these three areas that all contribute to the process of subjectification that is completed in adolescence. Piera Aulagnier (1975), in considering what she called the "I" (*le Je*), similarly alluded to the vitally important period of adolescence. At the end of this time, a balance is achieved involving self-esteem and a relatively stable cathexis of self- and object-representations, on the one hand, and, on the other, relative instinctual freedom, with a lesser subjection to pressures from the id, the superego, and the outside world.

What I am concerned with is the factors that prevent this kind of development; the pathology of subjectification. Patients who have managed the kind of development I have described are those whom psychoanalysts see on the couch, who can undergo the kind of treatment Freud described. They have managed to steer around the cape of adolescence without major mishap. But others have encountered difficulties that have caused the process of subjectification to remain disturbed. Their defensive systems are not such that, like the rest of us, they can attempt to represent themselves, to symbolize, to create and understand metaphor, to reflect upon themselves in a manner that allows them to confront the unknown part of themselves and engage in the search for as good a solution or means of understanding themselves as possible. That is what the rest of us attempt to do as best we can, in spite of all our conflicts and repressions, in spite of the part of ourselves that always escapes us and causes us to pursue a desire that eludes us just as we think we have it in our grasp. This is the process of subjectification that begins at birth, with Winnicott's subjective object, and continues until death. It does not end with adolescence: it continues indefinitely, but an essential part of the work has been completed. The adolescent is able to fulfil the internal need to have a viewpoint of his own, to take possession of his sexual body, to use his creative capacities, which include the capacity to symbolize and to organize and enrich a functioning pre-conscious. This means that he has been able to disengage from the power of the other, from the constraints of the outside world, from internal imperatives. He has achieved a way of being that is his own, through being forced to contain and to organize the changes that have impinged on him and made him into another person even while he remains himself. As Piera Aulagnier noted, the dialectic between continuity and change, the capacity to engage with both, indicate the end of adolescence in the least bad way possible.

What happens in other circumstances? In analytic treatment, we could say that we manage to reduce the burden imposed by the superego, to make the ego a bit more open to the id, to itself and to the world. Some sort of subject exists, the capacity for subjectification exists, alongside the analytic and emotional work. But sometimes this subject is absent or too weak, and, as always in Freudian thought, pathology teaches us what should have taken place but could not. Here is a simple example: a patient on the couch elaborates an ambivalent transference relationship with indications of hatred linked to the transference, to his personal history and images. You try to interpret with more or less difficulty. Bit by bit he realizes what is happening, he subjectivates, he becomes aware of a new link, a link which was there before but which he had never yet made. All this seems quite obvious. But if things go wrong, he will answer, "Not at all, Sir, I hate you because there is good reason to: you actually are a horrible person." In this situation there is no possibility of another viewpoint, of distinguishing between objective reality and symbolization or interpretation: in Winncott's terms, in these pathologies of subjectification, the therapist cannot be used as an object. Why is this? I believe it raises the possibility of a third formulation, beyond the two formulations of classical psychoanalysis which concern ego/id/superego and unconscious/preconscious/conscious. These remain as relevant as ever, but they are of no use if your interpretations cannot be heard and subjectified. Something has interfered with self–other differentiation, something has not allowed internal psychic reality to be differentiated from external reality. The original undifferentiated system of two-in-one, which one could call primary narcissism, in which the subjective object at the same time corresponds to hallucinatory wish-fulfilment and is an object external to the self, has not undergone differentiation. It is only with the recognition of the external object that we leave this totally subjective universe. This is what Freud explained so well: the object is born of hatred, and this is what brings about differentiation. Winnicott seems to have shown that things happen somewhat differently. This discovery of the separateness of the external world deserves to be called a genuine creation. The object no longer obeys the child's omnipotence: it is destroyed, it disappears, but there is no retaliation. A separate external world can open up, and the child is able to relinquish his former absolute omnipotence and to recognize the existence of the objective object. There exists a necessary condition: one area must remain under the sway of omnipotence without this being truly the case. This is the transitional space, of which one cannot be sure whether it is internal or external, whether it has been invented or whether it really exists in the outside world. This is the area in which we work in therapy, and where we do not need to know whether it derives from inside or outside. However, if the object has not been able to provide the reassurance, the basic security, that allows the gradual differentiation of self and object; or if the phase when self and object were undifferentiated involved intolerable suffering; or, conversely, if the mother's glance or attitude were so intrusive, so insistent, imperative, and alienating that no transitional space could be created; then the conditions in which subjectification can be achieved do not exist. This is the pathological constellation that we can observe in the most serious psychoses as well as in more or less severe borderline conditions. I believe that the capacity—or lack of capacity—for subjectification comprises a spectrum involving all degrees of what can or cannot be subjectified in each person's characteristic problems. We may encounter splitting, denial, projection, or projective identification; we may witness somatization, which is the inverse of mentalization. Indeed, splitting means that the left hand does not know what the right hand is doing, and it prevents a link from being established between the two: it is the mechanism that blocks subjectification from the beginning of our work, and we must seek to undo its effects.

How can we manage this? We may suppose the existence of a "subjectal" period prior to the capacity for subjectification, that is, a period of organization, of structuring, in which a self can exist in relation to an object. Following on from such a "subjectal" period, conditions for the process of subjectification may exist. If so, then things will take their course more or less successfully, which means that transference can exist and interpretations are possible to make.

Here is another example: you may show a psychotic his incestuous impulses, but we all know that this will achieve nothing, that there is no point, that no progress will come of it. Then there is the similar, but more complicated situation of the "as if" personalities described by Helene Deutsch. People with "as if" personalities—people like you and me, perhaps—have an analysis, and they understand everything. But the interpretations are like water off a duck's back. What has taken place? The meaning was understood, the transference was established, the infantile neurosis unfolded; and yet something did not happen: there was a split. It makes for a kind of invisible, transparent membrane, and the subject does not "realize" anything on a deep level, even if he is sincere. He thinks he has understood something, even integrated it, but nothing has moved. I believe this is a serious pathology of subjectification: all the more serious for being completely invisible. Now, I believe that this picture in the adult became definitively and irreversibly organized during adolescence. I am not talking about autism or childhood psychoses: these are another area. But it is not without reason that adolescence is the time when acute psychotic manifestations appear, which may or may not be reversible; and that this is also the time during which the personality is organized, more or less reversibly, into modes of functioning that we can observe later, on the couch, in a considerable proportion of the patients we see nowadays—that is, borderline patients. This is no longer Freud's (1915a) model of psychoanalytic treatment, as in that famous 1915 paper where he sets out what happens: you start an analysis, and the transference neurosis appears and develops. It's practically the equivalent of the infantile neurosis: a new illness, an elaboration, like a laboratory experiment. It's a new space where something is actualized that did not exist elsewhere: it is relived and understood at the same time. This is fairly amazing: a kind of miracle takes place; the truth is therapeutic. We say that the subject discovers what was hidden from him; that he discovers *his* truth; and that he is cured by means of interpretation. I shall be a bit provocative, and say that interpretation of the transference is our daily bread. That is what makes us psychoanalysts and distinguishes us, quite radically, from other psychotherapists. (That, and our concern with splitting, projective identification, denial, lack of verbalization.) For example, what do the psychosomaticists do? They no longer interpret, they don't argue about meaning. They may try to stimulate psychic activity, they try to elicit associations, thoughts, links, to help the subject to emerge from the realm of facts. They help him bit by bit to observe himself, to notice himself operating in one realm of discourse or another; for such a patient, this is an extraordinary discovery. In this way, psychosomaticists, even if they do not say so, are trying to establish a process of subjectification.

Perhaps some of you, like me, attended the workshop where we heard a fascinating presentation on a borderline adolescent. We heard a very talented analyst discuss this highly disturbed and perverse boy who was caught up in drug addiction; in destructive behaviour towards himself and his surroundings; in a truly terrifying inhibition of his development. We heard about the extraordinary piece of work she carried out—and it seemed to be analytic work, since she used the transference and looked for meaning, including the workings of projective identification and links between this adolescent's history and experience. But, in the end, what did she say? She said the same as Melanie Klein, that is, "after so many years and so many interpretations, after an extraordinary trial of strength in the course of which the counter-transference was elicited to the most taxing degree, the two things I have managed to achieve are the search for lost good objects and the possibility of containing fears of fragmentation." In other words, this work was not really concerned with meaning. I realize that I am being provocative; but this is not psychoanalytic work in the sense in which Freud defined it in 1915 in his paper on transference neurosis: it is work involving restitution. It's the kind of therapeutic work where the important thing is a corrective emotional experience, that is, that the therapist should be capable of containment. This is my hypothesis, not a postulate. And this implies that, at the very beginning, something went wrong between the child and his object. I could not agree at all with the therapist who made the astonishing suggestion that this boy's enormous intolerance of separation—with fears of death and an uprush of violence that completely took him over—came about through the birth of his little sister. A suggestion like that really puzzles me. I really believe that what happened to this boy at adolescence was the revival of the most primitive anxieties. Everything was to do with issues of identity, of the capacity to cohere internally, of a narcissistic foundation for all the subtle developments, the differentiations of object relationships and of identifications that characterize adolescence. For these developments to take place, the foundation has to be sufficiently solid, and in the case of this boy, it wasn't. He collapsed, and the most primitive anxieties of his life history resurfaced.

In my opinion, there are two significant dimensions to every treatment, whether the patient is a psychotic adolescent, a borderline adolescent, an adolescent who appears to be neurotic, or an adult: I'm not talking about children. I'm suggesting that there is the dimension of *subjectalization* and the dimension of *subjectification.* The dimension of subjectalization concerns everything to do with the setting, with containment; it concerns the essential importance of our maintaining continuity, of our availability, of a presence that is not the same as kindness: a kind of calm acceptance of the other as he is and in a way he can sense. It concerns an essential kind of listening: as attentive and benevolent as possible, but, above all, distinct from the characteristics of the object that may have been the most catastrophic or pathogenic. I do not believe that this means blaming the family. I am not an "anti-psychiatrist", and we know what happens in transgenerationally-based pathologies: how the parents themselves are invaded by happenings they are not responsible for, so that they are caught up in a repetition compulsion to act out traumas that were not their own. Or else there may have been a war in which the parents lost their own parents, or the mother lost her husband, so that it was simply not possible to focus sufficiently on the child. Things are infinitely more complicated than a schematic focus on blame might suggest. Nevertheless, the perspective I am outlining does imply that the role of the environment absolutely determines the outcome in matters of subjectalization.

On the other hand, when we focus on what happens in transitional space or in object relationships, we should behave as psychoanalysts: we should be ourselves in the sense of being a transference object: we should be completely paranoid: everything is aimed at us, and we need to return it to the patient in a way he can accept, so that he can acknowledge his own part in what is being re-enacted. This process concerns the generation of metaphor: it concerns subjectification, the use of the object. But when this process is interrupted, because A cannot be linked to B, because there is a confusion between self and object, then how can you explain to someone that I (in the role of B) am really the C that he has in his mind, since he can't distinguish A from B in the first place? He may see no clear difference between the two, and any capacity he may have for making distinctions may not operate vertically, between self and other, but horizontally, with a good part and a bad part inside the self that are projected "horizontally" on to the other. Well, I think that in this situation the patient will not be able to take this on board from his own felt perspective as a subject unless you react differently from the way he expected you to. That is essential, as Winnicott has emphasized, because it means that he has not been able to affect you unduly. When subject and object become separate, the subject can discover bit by bit that the object no longer responds in the same way as during the period when it was experienced as all-powerful, and necessarily either all good or all bad. Now things can be seen to be more complicated: there can be other perspectives besides omnipotence and lack of differentiation.

In my view, the therapeutic process in psychoanalytically based institutions for seriously disturbed or psychotic adolescents—those whose problems lie precisely in the area of subjectification—is not all that different from what takes place in individual work. Again, there are two fundamental dimensions that have to be addressed before, one day, "classical" treatment may become possible. First, a constant setting must be maintained come what may: a setting and a stance that do not yield to the patient's unconscious provocations or to the confusional system of interactions in which he is trapped. It is virtually impossible not to react at times, whether by being aggressive and rejecting, or else by being seductive or incestuous, which is no better. For example, one can become fascinated by the psychotic patient's material and get so caught up in the interaction that one can't tell who is thinking what. The essential thing is to keep to the setting, and, above all, to be aware of the very particular kind of countertransference that is operating. This is different from the countertransference manifestations that we are all familiar with. In the circumstances I am referring to, countertransference pressures can cause the therapist to be caught up in a repetition compulsion in which, without being aware of it, he is pushed to re-enact those unconscious circumstances that in the past contributed to the patient's psychosis. The essential thing is to be able to process and conceptualize these countertransference responses—not to interpret them: verbalization, like all symbolic function, is still light years away from where the patient is. Some therapists may not feel bothered by their reaction: this is a measure of the degree to which they remain caught up in a confusional process that they do not understand. At some point a "truth" is constructed that may be true or not—ultimately perhaps it does not matter, though I do think it is important that it should be as nearly true as possible. The essential thing is that something emerges for the therapist out of all this confusion, and that he can ascribe a meaning to it. If he finds a way out of this incomprehensible interactive magma, I believe that this movement is therapeutic in itself; infinitely more so than any verbal intervention. One may have understood something by means of the countertransference; a different way of applying this understanding will not be possible until a later stage. Winnicott gives clinical examples in which this dimension of *subjectalité* may dominate part of a session, and where, five minutes later, you may find yourself in the "objectal" transference in which classical interpretation becomes possible. This happens with borderline patients; it is an area where hatred and exasperation towards the patient are difficult to avoid. There are some situations where one is constantly moving between registers. On the level of technique as well as of theory, it is important to have the two poles of subjectification and subjectalization in mind, the better to understand this diffficult profession of ours.

[Question from the floor: I wonder whether it is possible to apply this to forensic cases where a therapeutic need emerges].

Raymond Cahn: I should tell you that I did not coin the term "subjectification": it has a long history of use by Ferenczi, Lacan and others, and also by Claude Balier, whom I do not know, but whose work in the areas you mention I very much admire. He has set up services in prisons along the lines of our day hospitals. What I think he achieves, at least for those patients who are not psychotic but who act out, is the possibility of some degree of mentalization. In that respect, his work and mine have similar objectives.

[Question from the floor: With regard to parental interactions during adolescence that you discuss in your book, one could re-phrase Winnicott's dictum that there is no such thing as a baby without a mother, and suggest that there is no such thing as an adolescent without parents. What precisely do you think is the role of parents during adolescence, and how could one conceptualize the part they play in the presence or absence of pathological episodes?]

Raymond Cahn: This is such a vast field that it is difficult for me to respond adequately. Sometimes conflicts that are characteristic of adolescence can indeed lead to a "decompensation"; sometimes it is as though adolescence occurred within a particular context that leads inexorably to problems. For example, if a father has a massively incestuous attitude (in Racamier's sense) which is completely unconscious, completely denied, this may not be much of an issue during his daughter's childhood: at most, she may appear a bit inhibited or featherbrained. But during adolescence, precisely the girl whose personality is more firmly established will find it intolerable to remain her father's little girl, who can never become an autonomous feminine sexual being. She can't protest or be rebellious because everything is so denied, everything seems to be going so well. Her only solution may be to construct a delusional system, both as a means of protesting and also to explain what she can't explain otherwise: that her father, who is so wonderful, makes it impossible for her to exist.

François Marty: To conclude, I want to refer you an idea Raymond Cahn put forward in his most recent book, *Adolescents in Psychoanalysis: the Adventure of Subjectification* (Cahn, 1998). He proposed that today adolescence has become the prototype of psychopathology, just as hysteria was in the nineteenth century. It concerns not just neurosis, but also, and more particularly, narcissistic and borderline pathologies, and all those syndromes where there are difficulties in self-representation. This, I think, is what Raymond Cahn has invited us to consider.

REFERENCES

Alvarez, A. (1992). *Live Company Psychoanalytic Psychotherapy with Autistic, Borderline, Deprived and Abused Children*. London: Routledge.

Alvarez, A. (1998). Failures to link: attacks or defects? Some questions concerning the thinkability of Oedipal and pre-Oedipal thoughts. *Journal of Child Psychotherapy, 24*: 213–232.

Alvarez, A. (1999). Disorder, deviance and personality: factors in the persistence and modifiability of autism. In: A. Alvarez & S. Reid (Eds.), *Autism and Personality: Findings from the Tavistock Autism Workshop*. London: Routledge.

Alvarez, A. (2004). Issues in assessment: Asperger's syndrome and personality. In M. Rhode & T. Klauber (Eds.), *The Many Faces of Asperger's Syndrome*. Tavistock Clinic Book Series, London: Karnac.

Alvarez, A., & Reid, S. (Eds.) (1999). *Autism and Personality: Findings from the Tavistock Autism Workshop*. London: Routledge.

American Psychiatric Association (1994). *Diagnostic and Statistical Manual of Mental Disorders* (4th edn). Washington, DC: American Psychiatric Association.

Anzieu, D. (1985). *Le Moi-peau*. Paris: Dunod.

Asperger, H. (1944). Die "autistischen Psychopathen" im Kindesalter. *Archiv für Psychiatrie und Nervenkrankheiten, 117*: 76–136. English edition: "Autistic psychopathy" in childhood (U. Frith, Trans.). In:

Frith, U. (Ed.), *Autism and Asperger Syndrome*. Cambridge: Cambridge University Press, 1991.
Aulagnier, P. (1975). *La Violence de l'Interprétation: Du Pictogramme à l'Énoncé*. Paris: PUF. English translation: *The Violence of Interpretation: From Pictogram to Statement*. Hove: Brunner-Routlege, 2001.
Balbernie, R. (2001). Circuits and circumstances: the neurobiological consequences of early relationship experiences and how they shape later behaviour. *Journal of Child Psychotherapy, 27*: 237–256.
Balint, M. (1968). *The Basic Fault: Therapeutic Aspects of Regression*. London: Tavistock.
Baron-Cohen, S., Leslie, A. M., & Frith, U. (1985). Does the autistic child have a "theory of mind"? *Cognition, 21*, 37–46.
Baron-Cohen, S., Cox, A., Baird, G., Swettenham, J., Nightingale, N., Morgan, K., Drew, A., & Charman, T. (1996). Psychological markers in the detection of autism in infancy in a large population. *British Journal of Psychiatry, 168*: 158–163.
Benedetti, G. (1983). *Psychosentherapie*. Stuttgart: Hippokrates.
Benedetti, G. (1992). *Psychotherapie als existentielle Herausforderung*. Göttingen: Vandenhoeck & Rupprecht.
Bettelheim, B. (1967). *The Empty Fortress*. New York: Free Press.
Bick, E. (1968). The experience of the skin in early object relations. *International Journal of Psychoanalysis, 49*: 484–486.
Bion, W. (1953). Notes on the theory of schizophrenia. In: *Second Thoughts* (pp. 23–35). New York: Jason Aronson, 1967.
Bion, W. R. (1957). Differentiation of the psychotic from the non-psychotic personalities. In: *Second Thoughts*. London: Heinemann, 1967.
Bion, W. R. (1959). Attacks on linking. In *Second Thoughts,* London: Heinemann, 1967.
Bion, W. (1962a). A theory of thinking. In: *Second Thoughts* (pp. 110–119). New York: Jason Aronson, 1967.
Bion, W. R. (1962b). *Learning from Experience*. London: Heinemann [reprinted, London: Karnac, 1984].
Bion, W. R. (1963). *Elements of Psychoanalysis*. London: William Heinemann.
Bleger, J. (1967). Psychoanalysis of the psychoanalytical frame. *International Journal of Psychoanalysis, 48*: 511–529.
Bowlby, J. (1953). Some pathological processes set in train by early mother–child separation. *Journal of Mental Sciences, 99*: 265–272.
Boyer, L. (1978). Countertransference experiences with severely regressed patients. *Contemporary Psychoanalysis, 14*: 48–71.

Brazelton, T. B., Koslowski, B., & Main, M. (1974). The origins of reciprocity: the early mother–infant interaction. In: M. Lewis & L. A. Rosenblum (Eds.), *The Effect of the Infant on its Caregivers*. London: Wiley Interscience.

Brazelton, T. B., Yogman, M., Als, H., & Tronick, E. (1979). The infant as focus for family reciprocity. In: M. Lewis & L. A. Rosenblum (Eds.), *The Child and Its Family*. New York: Plenum Press.

Bremner, J., & Meltzer, D. (1975). Autism proper—Timmy. In: D. Meltzer, J. Bremner, S. Hoxter, D. Weddell, & I. Wittenberg, *Explorations in Autism*. Strath Tay, Perthshire: Clunie Press.

Bruner, J. S. (1968). *Processes of Cognitive Growth: Infancy*. Worcester, MA: Clark University Press.

Cahn, R. (1998). *L'Adolescent dans la Psychanalyse*. Paris: PUF.

Caper, R. (1999). *A Mind of One's Own*. London: Routledge.

Cassell Concise English Dictionary (1995). London: Cassell.

Cassirer, E. (1923, 1924, 1929). *Die Philosophie der symbolischen Formen* (3 vols). Oxford: Bruno Cassirer.

Chasseguet-Smirgel, J. (1986). *Sexuality and the Mind*. New York: New York University Press.

Damasio, A. (2000). *The Feeling of What Happens: Body, Emotion, and the Making of Consciousness*. London: William Heinemann.

Dawson, G., & Lewy, A. (1989). Arousal, attention, and socioemotional impairment of individuals with autism. In: G. Dawson (Ed.), *Autism: Nature, Diagnosis and Treatment*. New York: Guilford Press.

De Astis, G. (1997). Thoughts about the development of a potential space in the psychoanalytic treatment of infantile psychosis. *Journal of Child Psychotherapy, 23*: 351–372.

De Masi, F. (2001). The unconscious and psychosis. In: P. Williams (Ed.), *A Language for Psychosis* (pp. 69–97). London: Whurr.

Dorpat, T. L. (1990). Female homosexuality. In: C. W. Socarides & V. D. Volkan (Eds.), *The Homosexualities*. Madison, CT: International Universities Press.

Ekstein, R. (1976). General treatment philosophy of acting out. In: L. E. Abt & S. L. Weissman (Eds.), *Acting Out* (pp. 162–171). New York: Jason Aronson.

Freud, S. (1900a). *The Interpretation of Dreams. S.E., 4–5*. London: Hogarth.

Freud, S. (1905d). *Three Essays on the Theory of Sexuality. S.E., 7*: 130 London: Hogarth, 1962.

Freud, S. (1915a). Observations on transference love (Further recommendations on the technique of psycho-analysis, III). *S.E., 12*: 157–173.

Freud, S. (1926d). *Inhibitions, Symptoms and Anxiety. S.E., 20*. London: Hogarth.

Frith, U. (1989). *Autism: Explaining the Enigma*. Oxford: Blackwell.

Fromm-Reichmann, F. (1950). *Principles of Intensive Psychotherapy*, Chicago: University of Chicago Press.

Gergely, G. (2000). Reapproaching Mahler: New perspectives on normal autism, symbiosis, splitting and libidinal object constancy from cognitive developmental theory. *Journal of the American Psychoanalytical Association, 48*: 1197–1228.

Giovacchini, P. L. (1997). *Schizophrenia and Primitive Mental States*. Northvale, NJ: Jason Aronson.

Green, A. (1975). The analyst, symbolization and absence in the analytic setting. In: *On Private Madness*, Madison: International Universities Press, 1986.

Green, A. (1993). *The Work of the Negative*. London: Free Association Books.

Greenspan, S. I. (1997). *Developmentally Based Psychotherapy*. Madison, CT: International Universities Press.

Grotstein, J. S. (1980). A proposed revision of primitive mental states: Part I. *Contemporary Psychoanalysis, 16*: 479–546.

Grotstein. J. S. (1990). Nothingness, meaninglessness, chaos, and the "black hole". *Contemporary Psychoanalysis, 26*: 377–407.

Grotstein, J. (1997). One pilgrim's progress: notes on Frances Tustin's contributions to the psychoanalytic conception of autism. In: T. Mitrani & J. L. Mitrani (Eds.), *Encounters with Autistic States: A Memorial Tribute to Frances Tustin*. Northvale, NJ: Jason Aronson.

Haag, G. (1985). La mère et le bébé dans les deux moitiés du corps. *Neuropsychiatrie de l'Enfance et de l'Adolescence, 33*: 107–114.

Haag, G. (1991). Nature de quelques identifications dans l'image du corps. *Journal de la Psychanalyse de l'Enfant, 10*: 73–92.

Haag, G. (1997). Psychosis and autism: schizophrenic, perverse and manic-depressive states during psychotherapy. In: M. Rustin, M. Rhode, A. Dubinsky, & H. Dubinsky (Eds.), *Psychotic States in Children*. London: Duckworth.

Hartwell, C. E. (1996). The schizophrenogenic mother concept in American psychiatry. *Psychiatry, 59*: 274–297.

Hobson, P. (1991). Against the "theory of mind", *British Journal of Developmental Psychology, 9*: 33–51.

Hobson, R. P. (1993). *Autism and the Development of Mind*. Hove: Psychology Press.

Hobson, R. P. (2002). *The Cradle of Thought*. Basingstoke: Macmillan.

Hodges, S. (2004). A psychological perspective on theories of Asperger's syndrome. In: M. Rhode & T. Klauber (Eds.), *The Many Faces of Asperger's Syndrome*. London: Karnac.

Hopper, E. (1991). Encapsulation as a defence against the fear of annihilation. *International Journal of Psychoanalysis, 72*: 607–624.

Houzel, D. (2000). Working with parents of autistic children. In: J. Tsiantis, S. Boalt Boëtius, B. Hallerfors, A. Horne, & L. Tischler (Eds.), *Work with Parents: Psychoanalytic Psychotherapy with Children and Adolescents*. EFPP Clinical Monograph Series. London: Karnac.

Houzel, D. (2001). The "nest of babies" fantasy. *Journal of Child Psychotherapy, 27*: 125–138.

Jackson, M., & Williams, P. (1994). *Unimaginable Storms*. London: Hogarth Press, 1975.

Jones, E. (1927). The early development of female sexuality. *International Journal of Psychoanalysis, 8*: 459–472.

Joseph, B. (1982). Addiction to near death. In: M. Feldman & E. B. Spillius (Eds.), *Psychic Equilibrium and Psychic Change: Selected Papers of Betty Joseph*. London: Tavistock/Routledge.

Josephs, L. (1989). The world of the concrete—a comparative approach. *Contemporary Psychoanalysis, 25*: 477–500.

Kanner, L. (1943). Autistic disturbance of affective contact. *Nervous Child, 2*: 217–50. Reprinted in L. Kanner: *Childhood Psychosis: Initial Studies and New Insights*. New York: Wiley, 1973.

Kaplan-Solms, K., & Solms, M. (2000). *Clinical Studies in Neuro-Psychoanalysis: Introduction to a Depth Neuropsychology*. London: Karnac.

Klauber, T. (1999). The significance of trauma and other factors in work with the parents of children with autism. In: A. Alvarez & S. Reid (Eds.), *Autism and Personality: Findings from the Tavistock Autism Workshop*. London: Routledge.

Klaus, M. H., & Kennell, J. H. (1982). *Parent–Infant Bonding*. London: C. H. Mosby.

Klein, M. (1929). Personification in the play of children. In: *The Writings of Melanie Klein, Vol. 1: Love, Guilt and Reparation and Other Works, 1921–1945* (pp. 199–209). London: Hogarth Press, 1975.

Klein, M. (1930). The importance of symbol-formation in the development of the ego. In: *The Writings of Melanie Klein, Vol. 1: Love, Guilt and Reparation and Other Works, 1921–1945* (pp. 219–232). London: Hogarth Press, 1975.

Klein, M. (1946). Notes on some schizoid mechanisms. In: *The Writings of Melanie Klein, Vol. 3: Envy and Gratitude and Other Works*. London: Hogarth Press, 1975.

Kristeva, J. (1982). *The Power of Horror.* New York: Columbia University Press.

Kurz, G. (1997). *Metapher, Allegorie, Symbol.* Göttingen: Vandenhoeck & Rupprecht, 1997.

Langer, S. K. (1942). *Philosophy in a New Key. A Study in the Symbolism of Reason, Rite and Art.* Cambridge, MA: Harvard University Press, 1979.

Laufer, M., & Laufer, M. E. (1984). *Adolescence and Developmental Breakdown: A Psychoanalytic View.* New Haven, CT: Yale University Press.

Leslie, A. M. (1987). Pretence and representation: the origins of theory of mind. *Psychological Review,* 94.

Lorenzer, A. (1970). *Zur Kritik des psychoanalytischen Symbolbegriffs.* Frankfurt: M Suhrkamp.

Mahler, M., Pine, F., & Bergman, A. (1975). *The Psychological Birth of the Human Infant.* New York: Basic Books.

Maiello, S. (1993). L'oggetto sonoro—Un'ipotesi sulle radici prenatali della memoria auditiva. *Richard e Piggle, 1*(1). English version (1995): The sound-object—a hypothesis about prenatal auditory experience and memory. *Journal of Child Psychotherapy,* 21: 23–91.

Maiello, S. (2000). Trames sonores et rythmiques primordiales. Réminiscences auditives dans le travail psychanalytique. *Journal de la Psychanalyse de l'Enfant,* 26: 77–103.

Maiello, S. (2001). Über das Fehlen rhythmischen Zeiterlebens im Autismus. In: *Zeit ohne Ende?—Aspekte der Zeitlichkeit in der psychoanalytischen Sozialarbeit.* Tübingen: Edition Diskord.

Meltzer, D. (1975a). Adhesive identification. *Contemporary Psychoanalysis, 11*: 289–310.

Meltzer, D. (1975b). The psychology of autistic states and of post-autistic mentality. In: D. Meltzer, J. Bremner, S. Hoxter, D. Weddell, & I. Wittenberg, *Explorations in Autism.* Strath Tay, Perthshire: Clunie Press.

Meltzer, D. (1994). *Sincerity and Other Works.* London: Karnac.

Meltzer, D., Bremner, J., Hoxter, S., Weddell, D., & Wittenberg, I. (1975). *Explorations in Autism.* Strath Tay, Perthshire: Clunie Press.

Miller, L., Rustin, M. E., Rustin, M. J., & Shuttleworth, J. (1989). *Closely Observed Infants.* London: Duckworth.

Milner, M. (1952). Aspects of symbolism in comprehension of the not-self. *International Journal of Psychoanalysis, 33*: 181–194.

Morin, E. (1991). De la complexité: complexus. In: F. Fogelman Soulié (Ed.), *Les théories de la complexité* (pp. 283–296). Paris: Seuil.

O'Connor, T., Rutter, M., & the English and Romanian Adoptees Study Team (2000). Attachment disorder behavior following early severe deprivation: Extension and longitudinal follow-up. *Journal of the American Academy of Child & Adolescent Psychiatry, 39*(6): 703–712.

Papousek, H., & Papousek, M. (1975). Cognitive aspects of preverbal social interaction between human infants and adults. In: *CIBA Foundation Symposium*. New York: Association of Scientific Publishers.

Perry, B., Pollard, R. A., Blakely, T. L., Baker, W. L., & Vigilante, D. (1995). Childhood trauma, the neurobiology of adaptation and "use-dependent" development of the brain: how states become traits. *Infant Mental Health Journal, 16*: 271–291.

Pestalozzi, J. (1996). Psychotische Übertragung als Chance—Psychotherapie eines dysmorfophoben Adoleszenten. *Kinderanalyse, 4*: 1–54.

Pestalozzi, J. (1999). Containment and the body of the analyst: on psychotic transference in adolescence. In: D. Anastasopoulos, E. Layiou-Lignos, & M. Waddell (Eds.), *Psychotherapy of the Severely Disturbed Adolescent*. London: Karnac.

Pestalozzi, J. (2000). Über therapeutische Symbiose. In: R. Battegay, E. Isler, & M. Nicola (Eds.), *Psychotherapie der Psychosen: Horizonte und Ausblicke*. Basel: F. Reinhardt, 2003.

Pestalozzi, J. (2001). Symbolisch und konkret. *Analytische Kinder- und Jugendlichenpsychotherapie*, 109: 63–88.

Piaget, J., & Inhelder, B. (1969). *The Psychology of the Child*. New York: Basic Books

Pine, F. (1983). A working nosology of borderline syndromes in children. In: K. Robson (Ed.), *The Borderline Child*. New York: McGraw-Hill.

Reid, S. (1997). *Developments in Infant Observation: The Tavistock Model*. London: Routledge.

Reid, S. (1999). Autism and trauma: autistic post-traumatic developmental disorder. In: A. Alvarez & S. Reid (Eds.), *Autism and Personality: Findings from the Tavistock Autism Workshop*. London: Routledge.

Resnik, S. (1986). *L'Expérience Psychotique*. Lyon: Césura Lyon Editions.

Resnik, S. (1990). *Spazio Mentale*. Turin: Bollati-Boringhieri editori. English edition: *Mental Space*, D. Alcorn (Trans.). London: Karnac, 1995.

Rey, J. H. (1979). Schizoid phenomena in the borderline. In: J. LeBoit & A. Capponi (Eds.), *Advances in the Psychotherapy of the Borderline Patient*. New York: Jason Aronson. Also in Spillius, E. B. (Ed.) *Melanie Klein Today: Vol. 1: Mainly Theory*, London/New York: Routledge, 1988.

Rhode, M. (1997). Going to pieces: autistic and schizoid solutions. In: M. Rustin, M. Rhode, A. Dubinsky, & H. Dubinsky (Eds.), *Psychotic States in Children*. London: Duckworth.

Rhode, M. (2000). Assessing children with communication disorders. In: M. Rustin & E. Quagliatia (Eds.), *Assessment in Child Psychotherapy*. London: Duckworth.

Rodrigué, E. (1956). Notes on symbolism. *International Journal of Psychoanalysis, 37*: 147–158.

Rosenfeld, H. (1952). Notes on the psycho-analysis of the superego conflict of an acute schizophrenic patient. *International Journal of Psychoanalysis, 33*: 111–131.

Rosenfeld, H. (1971). Contribution to the psychopathology of psychotic states. In: E. Bott Spillius (Ed.), *Melanie Klein Today, Volume 1*. London: Routledge, 1998.

Rosenfeld, H. (1987). *Impasse and Interpretation*. London: Tavistock.

Roth, P. (1998); *I Married a Communist*. London: Jonathan Cape.

Sacks, O. (1995). To see and not to see. In: *An Anthropologist on Mars*. London: Picador.

Sandler, A.-M., & Sandler, J. (1958). Psychoses, borderline states and mental deficiency in childhood. *Bulletin of the British Psychological Society*, 35.

Schmid Noerr, G. (2000). Symbolik des latenten Sinns. Zur psychoanalytischen Symboltheorie nach Lorenzer. *Psyche, 54*: 454–481.

Schore, A. N. (1994). *Affect Regulation and the Origin of the Self: The Neurobiology of Emotional Development*. Hillsdale, NJ: Lawrence Erlbaum.

Schore, A. N. (2001a). The effects of early relational trauma on right brain development, affect regulation, and infant mental health. *Infant Mental Health Journal, 22*: 201–269.

Schore, A. N. (2001b). The effects of a secure attachment relationship on right brain development, affect regulation and infant mental health. *Infant Mental Health Journal, 22*: 7–66.

Schore, A. N. (2002). (Communication during discussion). Conference on Trauma, Dissociation and Memory, at the Clinic for Dissociative Disorders, London.

Searles, H. E. (1968). *Collected Papers on Schizophrenia and Related Subjects*. London: Karnac.

Segal, H. (1957). Notes on symbol formation. *International Journal of Psychoanalysis*, *38*: 38–44.

Simpson, D., & Miller, L. (Eds.) (2004). *Unexpected Gains: Psychotherapy with People with Learning Disabilities*. London: Karnac.

Sinason, V. (1986). Secondary mental handicap and its relation to trauma. *Psychoanalytic Psychotherapy*, *2*: 131–154.

Solms, M., & Turnbull, O. (2002). *The Brain and the Inner World*. New York: Other Press.

Steiner, J. (1993). *Psychic Retreats*. London: Routledge.

Stern, D. (1974). Mother and infant at play: the dyadic interaction involving facial, vocal and gaze behaviours. In: M. Lewis & L. A. Rosenblum (Eds.), *The Effect of the Infant on its Caregivers*. London: Wiley Interscience.

Stern, D. N. (1985). *The Interpersonal World of the Infant: A View from Psychoanalysis and Developmental Psychology*. New York: Basic Books.

Sullivan, H. S. (1953). *The Interpersonal Theory of Psychiatry*. New York: W. W. Norton.

Thom, R. (1989). René Thom par lui-même. *PISTES*, *1*: June.

Trevarthen, C., Aitken, K., Papoudi, D., & Robarts, J. (1996). *Children with Autism: Diagnosis and Interventions to Meet Their Needs*. London: Jessica Kingsley (second revised edn, 1998).

Tronick, E. Z. (1989). Emotions and emotional communication in infants. *American Psychologist*, February, 112–119.

Tustin, F. (1972). *Autism and Childhood Psychosis*. London: Hogarth [reprinted London: Karnac, 1995].

Tustin, F. (1981a). Autistic objects. In: *Autistic States in Children*. London: Routledge (second revised edn, 1992).

Tustin, F. (1981b). *Autistic States in Children*. London: Routledge (second revised edn, 1992).

Tustin, F. (1990). *The Protective Shell in Children and Adults*. London: Karnac.

Tustin, F. (1991). What autism is and what autism is not. In: R. Szur & S. Miller (Eds.), *Extending Horizons. Psychoanalytic Psychotherapy with Children, Adolescents and Families*. London: Karnac.

Tustin, F. (1994). Autistic children who are assessed as not brain damaged. *Journal of Child Psychotherapy*, *20*: 103–132.

Urwin, C. (1987). Developmental psychology and psychoanalysis: splitting the difference. In: M. Richards & P. I. Light (Eds.), *Children in Social Worlds*. Cambridge: Polity Press.

Waddell, M. (1998). *Inside Lives. Psychoanalysis and the Growth of the Personality*. London: Duckworth.

Wing, L., & Attwood, A. (1987). Syndromes of autism and atypical development. In: D. Cohen & A. Donnellan (Eds.), *Handbook of Autism and Pervasive Developmental Disorders*. New York: Wiley.

Wing, L., & Gould, J. (1979). Severe impairments of social interactions and associated abnormalities in children: epidemiology and classification. *Journal of Autism and Developmental Disorders, 9*.

Winnicott, D. W. (1947). Hate in the countertransference. In: *Through Paediatrics to Psychoanalysis*. London: Hogarth, 1958 [reprinted London: Karnac, 1992].

Winnicott, D. W. (1963). The mentally ill in your caseload. In: *The Maturational Process and the Facilitating Environment*. London: Hogarth, 1965.

Winnicott, D. W. (1965). From dependence towards independence. In: *The Maturational Processes and the Facilitating Environment*. London: Hogarth.

Winnicott, D. W. (1966).The split-off male and female elements to be found in men and women. In: C. Winnicott, R. Shepherd, & M. Davis (Eds.), *Psycho-analytic Explorations*. London: Karnac, 1989.

Winnicott, D. W. (1974). Fear of breakdown. *International Review of Psycho-Analysis, 1*: 103–107.

World Health Organization (WHO) (1993). *International Classification of Diseases* (10th edn). Geneva: World Health Organization.

Youell, B. (1999). Matthew. From numbers to numeracy: from knowledge to knowing in a ten-year-old boy with Asperger´s syndrome. In: A. Alvarez & S. Reid (Eds.), *Autism and Personality. Findings from the Tavistock Autism Workshop*. London: Routledge.

INDEX

For Product Safety Concerns and Information please contact our EU
representative GPSR@taylorandfrancis.com
Taylor & Francis Verlag GmbH, Kaufingerstraße 24, 80331 München, Germany

www.ingramcontent.com/pod-product-compliance
Ingram Content Group UK Ltd.
Pitfield, Milton Keynes, MK11 3LW, UK
UKHW022201190926
475702UK00003B/142